Library of Congress Cataloging in Publication Data

Chilton Book Company. Automotive Editorial Dept.
    Chilton's new repair and tune-up guide for the Honda
twins.

    1. Honda motorcycle. I. Kelly, John D., ed.
II. Title. III. Title: New repair and tune-up guide
for the Honda twins.
TL448.H6C46   1972   629.28'7'75   72-7035
ISBN 0-8019-5736-2
ISBN 0-8019-5799-0 (pbk.)

ACKNOWLEDGMENTS

AMERICAN HONDA MOTOR COMPANY, INC.

Gardena, California

CHIACCIO MOTORS

Riverside, New Jersey

CHILTON'S *New* Repair and Tu

H

T

ILLUSTRATED

Prepared by the

Automotive Editorial Department

Chilton Book Company

401 Walnut Street
Philadelphia, Pa. 19106
215—WA 5-9111

managing editor **JOHN D. KELLY**
managing editor **PETER J. MEYER;**
tor, motorcycles **SVANTE E. MOSSE**
tors **James H. Johnson, Michael S.**

CHILTON BOOK COMPANY   PHILADELPHIA   NE\

1 · Model Identification and Description

Introduction

This book is intended to serve as a guide for the maintenance, tune-up and repair of the following Honda models:

CB 125 (from serial #4,000,001)
CL 125 (from serial #4,000,001)
CD 125 (from serial #2,000,001)
CB 175 (from serial #4,000,001)
CL 175 (from serial #4,000,001)
CD 175 (from serial #2,000,001)
SL 175 (1970 thru 1972)
CB 350 (1968 thru 1972)
CL 350 (1968 thru 1972)
SL 350 (1970)
SL 350K1 and K2 (1971 and 1972)
CB 450 (1966 thru 1969)
CL 450 (1968 and 1969)
CB 450K4 and K5 (1970 thru 1972)
CL 450K4 and K5 (1970 thru 1972)

To use it properly, one must approach each operation logically and read the recommended procedures thoroughly before actually beginning the work. It is also necessary, of course, to have the required tools and a clean, uncluttered place in which to do the work. Cleanliness is an item that cannot be overstressed and will be emphasized throughout the text.

Each chapter is constructed so that descriptions, procedures, and specifications can be easily located, thus allowing experienced mechanics to isolate only the information they will find useful, and yet provide the inexperienced mechanic with background data necessary to his understanding of the machine.

Development History

In 1948, when the Honda Motor Company was formed, Soichiro Honda was in the right place at the right time, and he made the right move. Post-war Japan was desperately in need of inexpensive transportation, and Honda's first product—a cheap, reliable motorized bicycle—filled this need admirably. The little moped incorporated a small Imperial-army-surplus two-stroke engine that ran on a fuel extracted from the roots of pine trees. It sold very quickly, and Honda's supply of engines was soon exhausted. Consequently, he designed his own engine, a 50 cc two-stroke, and it was such a success that production of the moped could not satisfy the demand.

The success and growth of his company, by 1949, enabled Honda to produce a completely Honda-designed motorcycle, and in August of that year, the 100 cc D model, which became known as the Dream, was introduced. The Dream featured a pressed steel frame with rigid rear suspension and telescopic front forks. Its 2.3 horsepower two-stroke engine drove through a two-speed transmission and a chain final drive. Unfortunately, at about this time, Japan was hit by an economic recession and the Honda Motor Company suffered to the point of near bankruptcy. Honda wisely hired a sales and financial director, since this was the weakest area in his organization, and by 1950, the company was showing increasing growth once again. Japan began her astounding industrial growth, and the Honda Motor Company increased its production very rapidly. By the end of 1950, Honda was producing 300 Dream models per month, compared to the 1,600 units per year that all other Japanese motorcycle manufacturers combined were producing.

Honda's first four-stroke motorcycle, the E model, was introduced early in the 1950s. Its 5.5 horsepower engine was mounted in a pressed steel frame much like that of the earlier D model, and it had a top speed of 50 mph. The E model was a huge success, with 32,000 of them sold in 1953.

May of 1952 saw the introduction of a new Honda moped, the 50 cc Cub. Production was soon up to 6,500 per month, and the fantastic sales of the Cub enabled Honda to plow an ever-increasing amount of money back into the company for research and development.

The 90 cc four-stroke Benly was designed and produced in 1953. The Benly was a much more modern bike than its predecessors, with a 3.8 horsepower engine

and three-speed foot-shift transmission. The pressed steel frame was all new, and it had telescopic suspension up front and torsion bar suspension at the rear.

The Honda Motor Company spent over one million dollars in 1953 on modern, efficient machine tools in anticipation of entering into the world market. Toward this end, Honda fielded a team for the 1954 Isle of Man TT races, hoping to compete with the European machines and pave the way for sales of Honda motorcycles in other countries. Honda's racing bikes were clearly uncompetitive and were beaten badly. All efforts were turned, for a time, on improving the line of street machines, and in 1955 several new models appeared. One of the most notable, the SA model, was an OHV 250 with swing arm rear suspension.

The most famous Honda motorcycle—the one that catapulted Honda into the world market—was the 50 cc Super Cub, introduced in 1958. It was soon followed by the overhead cam twins, which solidified Honda's position and helped to make Honda one of the largest motorcycle manufacturers in the world. Honda avenged the earlier defeat at the Isle of Man by building a series of extremely complex and powerful GP motorcycles that, during the early and middle 1960s, won every class of international road racing.

The present line of twin-cylinder Hondas includes 125 cc, 175 cc, 250 cc (not imported into the United States), 350 cc, and 450 cc machines. They all are fast, smooth, and very reliable.

General Specifications

Model	CB 125 (from serial no. 4,000,001)	CL 125 (from serial no. 4,000,001)
ENGINE		
Displacement (cc)	124	124
Bore and stroke (mm)	44 x 41	44 x 41
Compression ratio	9.4 : 1	9.4 : 1
Carburetion (Keihin)	(2) 18 mm	(2) 18 mm
Horsepower @ rpm	14.8 @ 10,000	13.8 @ 10,000
Torque (ft lb) @ rpm	7.59 @ 8,500	7.66 @ 8,500
Weight (lb)	77.2	68.4
DRIVE TRAIN		
Clutch type	wet, multi-plate	wet, multi-plate
Gear ratios:		
1st	2.692	2.615
2nd	1.667	1.611
3rd	1.286	1.190

General Specifications

Model	CB 125 (from serial no. 4,000,001)	CL 125 (from serial no. 4,000,001)
DRIVE TRAIN		
Gear ratios:		
4th	1.043	0.880
5th	0.880	——
Primary reduction	3.875	3.875
Final reduction	3.133	3.133
CHASSIS		
Weight (lb)	262	254
Wheelbase (in.)	50.4	50.4
Tire size (in.):		
front	2.50 x 18	2.75 x 18
rear	2.75 x 18	3.00 x 18
Overall length (in.)	77.9	76.0
Overall width (in.)	29.3	31.9
Overall height (in.)	40.9	40.6
Ground clearance (in.)	5.5	6.1
ELECTRICAL SYSTEM		
Ignition	battery and coil	battery and coil
Starting system	electric and kick	electric and kick
Charging system:		
battery (volts/amp hrs)	6/12	6/6
alternator	rotor type	rotor type
regulator	——	——

Model	SS 125 (from serial no. 2,000,001)	CB 175 (from serial no. 4,000,001)
ENGINE		
Displacement (cc)	124	174
Bore and stroke (mm)	44 x 41	52 x 41
Compression ratio	9.4 : 1	9.0 : 1
Carburetion (Keihin)	——	(2) 20 mm
Horsepower @ rpm	12.5 @ 10,000	19.8 @ 10,000
Torque (ft lb) @ rpm	6.8 @ 8,500	10.8 @ 8,500
Weight (lb)	75.0	88.2
DRIVE TRAIN		
Clutch type	wet, multi-plate	wet, multi-plate
Gear ratios:		
1st	2.615	2.769
2nd	1.611	1.882
3rd	1.190	1.450
4th	0.880	1.173
5th	——	1.000
Primary reduction	3.875	3.700
Final reduction	3.071	2.375
CHASSIS		
Weight (lb)	265	280
Wheelbase (in.)	50.4	50.4
Tire size (in.):		
front	3.00 x 17	2.75 x 18
rear	3.00 x 17	3.00 x 18
Overall length (in.)	78.0	78.4
Overall width (in.)	29.5	29.3
Overall height (in.)	40.2	40.9
Ground clearance (in.)	5.5	6.6
ELECTRICAL SYSTEM		
Ignition	battery and coil	battery and coil
Starting system	electric and kick	electric and kick
Charging system:		
battery (volts/amp hrs)	6/12	12/9
alternator	rotor type	rotor type
regulator	——	——

General Specifications

Model	CL 175 (from serial no. 4,000,001)	CD 175 (from serial no. 2,000,001)
ENGINE		
Displacement (cc)	174	174
Bore and stroke (mm)	52 x 41	52 x 41
Compression ratio	9.0 x 1	9.0 x 1
Carburetion (Keihin)	(2) 22 mm	
Horsepower @ rpm	19.8 @ 10,000	16.8 @ 9,500
Torque (ft lb) @ rpm	10.8 @ 8,500	9.4 @ 7,000
Weight (lb)	82.7	87.1
DRIVE TRAIN		
Clutch type	wet, multi-plate	wet, multi-plate
Gear ratios:		
1st	2.769	2.769
2nd	1.882	1.778
3rd	1.450	1.318
4th	1.173	1.040
5th	1.000	——
Primary reduction	3.700	3.700
Final reduction	2.470	2.294
CHASSIS		
Weight (lb)	274	271
Wheelbase (in.)	50.8	50.4
Tire size (in.):		
front	3.00 x 19	3.00 x 17
rear	3.00 x 18	3.00 x 17
Overall length (in.)	78.3	78.0
Overall width (in.)	32.3	29.5
Overall height (in.)	42.5	40.2
Ground clearance (in.)	7.8	6.1
ELECTRICAL SYSTEM		
Ignition	battery and coil	battery and coil
Starting system	electric and kick	electric and kick
Charging system:		
battery (volts/amp hrs)	12/9	6/12
alternator	rotor type	rotor type
regulator	——	——

Model	SL 175 (1970–72)	CB 350 (1968–72)
ENGINE		
Displacement (cc)	174	325
Bore and stroke (mm)	52 x 41	65 x 50.6
Compression ratio	9.0 : 1	9.5 : 1
Carburetion (Keihin)	——	(2) 28 mm CV
Horsepower @ rpm	20 @ 10,000	36 @ 10,500
Torque (ft lb) @ rpm	——	18.5 @ 9,500
Weight (lb)	——	115.5
DRIVE TRAIN		
Clutch type	wet, multi-plate	wet, multi-plate
Gear ratios:		
1st	2.769	2.353
2nd	1.882	1.636
3rd	1.450	1.269
4th	1.173	1.036
5th	1.000	0.900
Primary reduction	3.700	3.714
Final reduction	2.687	2.250
CHASSIS		
Weight (lb)	262.4	370.0
Wheelbase (in.)	51.6	52.0

General Specifications

Model	SL 175 (1970–72)	CB 350 (1968–72)
CHASSIS		
Tire size (in.):		
front	3.00 x 19	3.00 x 18
rear	3.50 x 17	3.50 x 18
Overall length (in.)	78.5	79.2
Overall width (in.)	30.7	30.5
Overall height (in.)	42.9	42.3
Ground clearance (in.)	——	5.9
ELECTRICAL SYSTEM		
Ignition	battery and coil	battery and coil
Starting system	kick	electric and kick
Charging system:		
battery (volts/amp hrs)	12/5	12/12
alternator	rotor type	rotor type
regulator	non-adjustable silicon type	non-adjustable silicon type

Model	CL 350 (1968–72)	SL 350 (1970)
ENGINE		
Displacement (cc)	325	325
Bore and stroke (mm)	64 x 50.6	64 x 50.6
Compression ratio	9.5 : 1	9.5 : 1
Carburetion (Keihin)	(2) 28 mm CV	(2) 28 mm CV
Horsepower @ rpm	33 @ 9,500	33 @ 9,500
Torque (ft lb) @ rpm	19.5 @ 8,000	19.5 @ 8,000
Weight (lb)	115.5	115.5
DRIVE TRAIN		
Clutch type	wet, multi-plate	wet, multi-plate
Gear ratios:		
1st	2.353	2.353
2nd	1.636	1.636
3rd	1.269	1.269
4th	1.036	1.036
5th	0.900	0.900
Primary reduction	3.714	3.714
Final reduction	2.375	2.500
CHASSIS		
Weight (lb)	366	364
Wheelbase (in.)	52.0	52.8
Tire size (in.):		
front	3.00 x 19	3.25 x 19
rear	3.50 x 18	4.00 x 18
Overall length (in.)	79.5	79.5
Overall width (in.)	32.7	33.3
Overall height (in.)	42.9	46.5
Ground clearance (in.)	7.1	8.3
ELECTRICAL SYSTEM		
Ignition	battery and coil	battery and coil
Starting system	electric and kick	electric and kick
Charging system:		
battery (volts/amp hrs)	12/12	12/12
alternator	rotor type	rotor type
regulator	non-adjustable silicon type	non-adjustable silicon type

Model	SL 350K1 and K2 (1971–72)	CB 450 (1966–67)
ENGINE		
Displacement (cc)	325	444
Bore and stroke (mm)	64 x 50.6	70 x 57.8

General Specifications

Model	SL 350K1 and K2 (1971–72)	CB 450 (1966–67)
ENGINE		
Compression ratio	9.5 : 1	8.5 : 1
Carburetion (Keihin)	(2) 24 mm	(2) 36 mm CV
Horsepower @ rpm	25 @ 8,000	43 @ 8,500
Torque (ft lb) @ rpm	18.1 @ 8,000	27.6 @ 7,250
Weight (lb)	103.5	146.6
DRIVE TRAIN		
Clutch type	wet, multi-plate	wet, multi-plate
Gear ratios:		
1st	2.353	2.411
2nd	1.636	1.400
3rd	1.280	1.034
4th	1.036	0.903
5th	0.900	——
Primary reduction	3.714	3.304
Final reduction	2.500	2.333
CHASSIS		
Weight (lb)	306.5	412
Wheelbase (in.)	54.7	53.2
Tire size (in.):		
front	3.25 x 19	3.25 x 18
rear	4.00 x 18	3.50 x 18
Overall length (in.)	83.07	82.0
Overall width (in.)	33.07	30.2
Overall height (in.)	45.08	53.2
Ground clearance (in.)	8.3	5.4
ELECTRICAL SYSTEM		
Ignition	battery and coil	battery and coil
Starting system	kick only	electric and kick
Charging system:		
battery (volts/amp hrs)	12/5.5	12/12
alternator	rotor type	rotor type
regulator	non-adjustable silicon type	——

Model	CB 450 (1968–69)	CL 450 (1968–69)
ENGINE		
Displacement (cc)	444	444
Bore and stroke (mm)	70 x 57.8	70 x 57.8
Compression ratio	9.0 : 1	9.0 : 1
Carburetion (Keihin)	(2) 36 mm CV	(2) 36 mm CV
Horsepower @ rpm	45 @ 9,000	43 @ 8,000
Torque (ft lb) @ rpm	28 @ 7,500	29 @ 7,000
Weight (lb)	137.8	137.8
DRIVE TRAIN		
Clutch type	wet, multi-plate	wet, multi-plate
Gear ratios:		
1st	2.412	2.412
2nd	1.636	1.636
3rd	1.269	1.269
4th	1.000	1.000
5th	0.844	0.844
Primary reduction	3.304	3.304
Final reduction	2.333	2.333
CHASSIS		
Weight (lb)	412	401
Wheelbase (in.)	54.0	54.0

General Specifications

Model	CB 450 (1968–69)	CL 450 (1968–69)
CHASSIS		
Tire size (in.):		
front	3.25 x 18	3.25 x 19
rear	3.50 x 18	3.50 x 18
Overall length (in.)	83.0	84.5
Overall width (in.)	30.5	32.5
Overall height (in.)	43.0	43.5
Ground clearance (in.)	5.5	6.0
ELECTRICAL SYSTEM		
Ignition	battery and coil	battery and coil
Starting system	electric and kick	electric and kick
Charging system:		
battery (volts/amp hrs)	12/12	12/12
alternator	rotor type	rotor type
regulator	non-adjustable silicon type	non-adjustable silicon type

Model	CB 450K4 and K5 (1970–72) *	CL 450K4 and K5 (1970–72)
ENGINE		
Displacement (cc)	444	444
Bore and stroke (mm)	70 x 57.8	70 x 57.8
Compression ratio	9.0 : 1	9.0 : 1
Carburetion (Keihin)	(2) 36 mm CV	(2) 36 mm CV
Horsepower @ rpm	45 @ 9,000	43 @ 8,000
Torque (ft lb) @ rpm	28 @ 7,500	29 @ 7,000
Weight (lb)	137.8	137.8
DRIVE TRAIN		
Clutch type	wet, multi-plate	wet, multi-plate
Gear ratios:		
1st	2.412	2.412
2nd	1.636	1.636
3rd	1.269	1.269
4th	1.000	1.000
5th	0.844	0.844
Primary reduction	3.304	3.304
Final reduction	2.333	2.333
CHASSIS		
Weight (lb)	430	414.5
Wheelbase (in.)	54.3	54.0
Tire size (in.):		
front	3.25 x 19	3.25 x 19
rear	3.50 x 18	3.50 x 18
Overall length (in.)	82.7	82.0
Overall width (in.)	30.5	32.7
Overall height (in.)	42.3	42.9
Ground clearance (in.)	5.7	7.1
ELECTRICAL SYSTEM		
Ignition	battery and coil	battery and coil
Starting system	electric and kick	electric and kick
Charging system:		
battery (volts/amp hrs)	12/12	12/12
alternator	rotor type	rotor type
regulator	non-adjustable silicon type	non-adjustable silicon type

* disc brake models

NOTE: Beginning in 1967, Honda (and many other manufacturers) began using nuts and bolts manufactured to the ISO metric standard rather than the earlier JIS standard that had been widely used in both Japan and Europe. ISO and JIS hardware is interchangeable in some sizes; however, the thread pitch in a few of the common sizes used has been changed and, in these cases, the hardware is not interchangeable. Note also that, except for the 10 mm size (6 mm diameter thread), the width (across flats) of size ISO nuts and bolts (relative to the thread diameter), has been reduced from that of JIS hardware. ISO parts are identified by an embossed dot on the bolt head or nut.

Interchangeability Chart

Thread Diameter	Width Across Flats		Thread Pitch	
	ISO	JIS	ISO	JIS
3 mm	5.5	6	0.5	0.6
4 mm	7	8	0.7	0.75
5 mm	8	9	0.8	0.9
6 mm	10-------10		1.0----1.0	
8 mm	12	14	1.25---1.25	
10 mm	14	17	1.25---1.25	
12 mm	17	19	1.25	1.5
14 mm	19	21	1.5----1.5	
16 mm	22	23	1.5----1.5	
18 mm	24	26	1.5----1.5	
20 mm	27	29	1.5----1.5	

2 · Maintenance

Introduction

The importance of maintaining a motorcycle conscientiously and carefully cannot be overstressed. Apart from the obvious benefits of safety and economy, a well-maintained bike will generally be ridden with more care and consideration than a dirty, out-of-tune motorcycle. When something is wrong with their machine, even something very minor, most riders tend to become annoyed and will treat the bike more harshly than they normally would. This, naturally, does nothing but aggravate the problem and may lead to component failure sooner than expected.

To counter the tendency toward frustration and anger when one's motorcycle is not right, a special attitude toward maintenance must be developed. If you stay aware and actually take notice of what you are doing, you can gain a sensitivity for your machine and know beforehand when something is wearing out or needs attention. Aircraft maintenance crews and professional racing mechanics use maintenance checklists and logbooks to make certain that no operations are overlooked and that no component is stressed beyond its maximum working life. They view maintenance as preventative action, rather than corrective action.

Motorcycle maintenance should be ap-

proached in basically the same manner. Keeping a machine properly serviced need not be excessively time consuming, but services should be performed regularly and in a professional manner. This means that the owner/mechanic should have:

1. An adequate supply of good quality tools.
2. A fairly clean place to work.
3. Enough time to do the job properly.
4. Necessary working specifications and procedures.

Just as in breaking-in a bike and getting acquainted with it, a feel should be developed for the maintenance needs of the various components. The conditions under which the machine is used will have a great bearing on when attention is necessary. It may be beneficial to modify the maintenance schedule after a few thousand miles have been covered and the bike's peculiarities have become known.

Daily Inspection

A daily inspection doesn't have to involve more than a quick "confirmation" check of the bike and should take no more than a few seconds. Items to be checked before each ride include:

1. Operation of the lights (especially the brake light).

2. Brake adjustment.
3. Engine oil level.

Weekly Inspection

In addition to the items that are checked daily, inspect and adjust, if necessary:

1. Tire pressure.
2. Chain adjustment.
3. Battery electrolyte level.
4. Clutch adjustment.
5. Lubricate control cables and pivots.
6. Tightness of critical nuts and bolts such as axle nuts, engine mounting bolts, and control fasteners.

It would be a good idea to clean the bike as thoroughly as time permits, even if it is only to hose it down and wipe it dry. A motorcycle can accumulate an amazing amount of dirt in a short time and, if it is allowed to build up for more than a few weeks, it will take hours to clean. If the bike is taken to a car wash with high-pressure spray equipment, be careful to keep the spray away from the air filter, carburetors, and wheel bearings—hot water under pressure can work itself into all kinds of places where it shouldn't be. Remember to check the brakes after washing, as water can make them useless on the first few applications. Drag them slightly, if necessary, to dry them out. Start and run the engine for at least ten minutes to evaporate any water that has accumulated in vital areas.

Periodic Maintenance

ENGINE

Oil Changes (1,000 mi / 60 days summer, 30 days winter)

In any high-performance engine, the oil plays a vital part in maintaining smooth, trouble-free running and longevity. Not only does the oil lubricate moving parts but it must also act as a coolant, which is especially important in an air-cooled engine.

Honda recommends that the oil initially be changed at 200–600 miles and there-after at 1,000 mile intervals. However, frequent oil changes are excellent life insurance for any engine, and some discretion should be exercised on the part of the rider as to when the oil *needs* to be changed. For example, during the first 2,000 miles, the engine will be tighter, run hotter, and have more abrasive particles in the oil than at any time in its life. Accordingly, changing the oil at, say, 500 mile intervals during this period would be wise. If the motorcycle is ridden in stop and go traffic or cold weather, again the oil should be changed more frequently to prevent acids and condensation that accumulate during this kind of service from corroding the engine or diluting the oil.

Change the oil after the engine has been run long enough to be up to operating temperature. This ensures that the oil is fluid enough to drain completely and that impurities suspended in the oil while it is circulating will be removed. Honda recommends that SAE 10W-40 or 10W-50 oil of SD (previously MS) service rating be used. For even better protection, you can use the new SE rated oils, which are able to withstand more heat than SD rated oil before breaking down. If a single-viscosity oil is to be used, it must be a high detergent (heavy duty) oil of SD service rating. For temperatures above 60°F, use SAE 30W-30 oil; between 32 and 60°F, use SAE 20W-20; and below 32°F, use SAE 10W-10 oil. Do not use a vegetable-based or nondetergent oil.

Remove the drainplug from the crankcase sump and remove the filler cap to assist draining. When most of the oil has drained, kick the engine over a few times to remove any oil remaining in the delivery system. Replace the drainplug and re-

Oil drain plug (1).

fill the engine with the correct grade and amount of oil. Start the engine and let it idle for a minute or so to circulate the oil. Shut the engine off and check the oil level with the filler dipstick. To obtain a true reading on the dipstick, three precautions must be observed:

1. Allow the oil a few seconds to drain down into the crankcase.

2. Place the machine on its center stand, on a level surface.

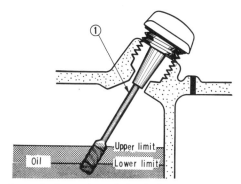

When checking the oil level do not screw the dipstick (1) into the crankcase.

3. Do not screw the dipstick/filler cap into the case when checking the oil level or a false (high) reading will be obtained. Add oil, if necessary, to bring the level to the upper mark on the dipstick.

Oil Filter (3,000 mi)

A centrifugal oil filter is used on all models. The filter does not need to be cleaned at every oil change, but it should be cleaned at regular intervals (twice a year, or about every sixth oil change on machines that are used daily and accumulate high mileages).

1. Clean the oil filter in conjunction with an oil change. Drain the oil and do not reinstall the drain plug at this time.

2. Take out the three screws and remove the small circular cover plate at the right side of the engine towards the front.

3. Remove the circlip and gently pull the rotor cap out of the oil filter rotor.

NOTE: *On early 450s the rotor cap is held in place with an aluminum bolt rather than a circlip. When removing and installing the bolt, take great care not to apply sudden or excessive torque to it, as it can be broken off very easily.*

4. Clean the inside of the filter rotor with solvent or gasoline and allow the

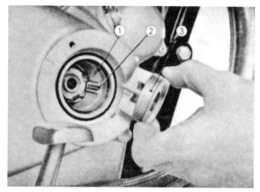

Removing the oil filter rotor cap, showing the rotor (1), rotor cap alignment groove (2), and rotor cap (3).

cleaning agent to drain completely before replacing the oil drain plug. Clean the rotor cap and cover plate, and dry thoroughly.

5. Install the rotor cap with the vanes located in the grooves on the inside of the rotor, and secure with the circlip. Before installing the cover plate, check that the oil guide in the center of the plate (if applicable) is free to operate smoothly and that the gasket or O-rings are in good con-

Checking the operation of the oil guide (1). Some models do not have an oil guide.

With the rotor cap (1) in place, install the cover plate (2) so that its oil holes (3) align with the holes in the crankcase cover.

dition. Install the cover plate so that the matching holes in the plate and crankcase cover are aligned. Install the drainplug and refill the engine with oil.

Air Filter (3,000 mi / 6 mo)

The air filter element should be serviced without fail at the prescribed intervals, or more frequently under dusty conditions. A dirty filter can cause poor running, excessive fuel consumption and carbon buildup, and, ultimately, overheating.

On all models, the filter elements are located within the side panels. On machines with paper elements, clean, using compressed air (directed from the inside out) or by tapping the elements lightly and brushing away the dirt. Replace the elements if they are torn or wet with oil or water. On machines with rubber foam type filter elements, clean in solvent and wet the elements with oil. Wring out any excess oil before reinstalling. Replace the elements if torn.

Clutch Adjustment (3,000 mi / 6 mo)

The clutch release mechanism should be adjusted at the prescribed intervals, or whenever the clutch begins to drag or slip and satisfactory operation cannot be obtained by adjusting free-play at the lever. At the time of adjustment, lubricate the grease fitting, using only one or two strokes of the grease gun.

1. Screw the cable adjuster at the clutch lever all the way into the lever (increasing lever free-play).

2. Back off the locknut and turn the cable adjuster at the engine case into the case (increasing cable free-play to maximum).

3. Loosen the clutch adjuster locknut or bolt, and turn the adjuster clockwise (125,

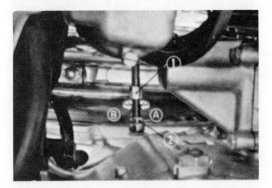

Bottom cable adjuster bolt (1) and locknut (2).

175, and 450) or counterclockwise (350) until resistance is felt. Then turn the adjuster in the opposite direction about $\frac{1}{8}$–$\frac{1}{4}$ in. ($\frac{1}{2}$ turn on the 350) and retighten the locknut or bolt.

NOTE: *On the 350, if a loud click is heard and the cable goes slack (or if the cable goes slack for no apparent reason while riding), turn the lower cable adjuster into the engine case a few more turns and reset the adjuster screw.*

Clutch adjuster (1) and lockbolt (2), all except 350.

Clutch adjuster (1) and locknut (2), 350.

4. Turn the cable adjuster at the engine case out until there is about 1–2 in. free-play at the end of the clutch lever.

5. Remaining adjustment is made at the lever. Free-play at the end of the lever should be 0.4–0.8 in.

BATTERY

The battery is located beneath the flip-up seat (late models) or behind the side panel (earlier models). Electrolyte level can be checked through the clear battery case. If necessary, add distilled water to raise the electrolyte level to a position between the upper and lower marks. *Do not overfill.*

Battery electrolyte level maximum mark (1) and minimum mark (2).

CAUTION: *Exercise extreme care in handling the battery. Electrolyte can remove paint and chrome in seconds, as well as cause skin burns. Baking soda can be used, if necessary, as a neutralizer.*

Check the condition of the battery breather tube. It must extend to a point below the frame where relatively little damage can be done if the battery spills or boils over. Make sure that the tube is not pinched or closed off, or the battery may build up enough pressure to explode.

Battery charge should be checked periodically with a hydrometer. If the specific gravity reading on any cell is below 1.200 (at 68°F), the battery should be recharged. Do not use a high-output battery charger unless absolutely necessary. If the battery must be charged quickly, observe these precautions:

1. Do not charge the battery at an amperage rate greater than its rated amp/hr capacity.

2. Never allow electrolyte temperature to exceed 110°F while charging.

3. Do not quick-charge a fully discharged battery.

4. Do not charge the battery in a confined room or near heat, as hydrogen gas is released during charging.

5. Do not quick-charge a battery in which the specific gravity of one or more cells is noticeably lower than the others.

6. Disconnect the positive battery cable if the battery is to be charged while on the motorcycle.

7. Thirty minutes is usually adequate charging time at maximum charging rate.

An alternative to the high-output charger is an adjustable low-output charger, available at most automotive supply stores at reasonable cost. A battery that is charged at a low rate will take and retain a fuller charge, and plate damage due to high current input is less likely to occur. When charging a battery at a low rate, observe item 6 above, and do not exceed the following charging rates:

6 AH battery—2.0 amps
9 AH battery—2.7–3.0 amps
12 AH battery—3.6–4.0 amps

Do not charge a battery for an extended period of time at a rate of charge greater than $\frac{1}{10}$ its amp/hr (AH) rating.

When rechecking specific gravity of the cells after charging, allow sufficient time for the gas bubbles to be released or a false (low) reading will be obtained. A good battery should have a specific gravity reading in all cells of between 1.260–1.280 at 68°F. The battery should be replaced if one or more cells is excessively low. If charging system fault is suspected, refer to chapter 7.

Do not neglect to keep the battery case and terminals clean. A solution of baking soda and water works well to remove corrosion. Be careful not to let it enter the cells or the electrolyte will be neutralized. Petroleum jelly can be used as a corrosion inhibitor on the terminals after they have been cleaned.

FUEL SYSTEM (3,000 mi/6 mo)

The fuel filter, located in the fuel tap, should be removed and cleaned at the prescribed intervals or whenever fuel feed problems are suspected. Simply turn the fuel tap to "stop" and unscrew the cup to gain access to the filter. Fuel flow at both the "on" and "reserve" positions can be checked at this time.

CAUTION: *Do not start the engine until all spilled gasoline has evaporated or has been wiped off the engine. Use a can or jar to catch gasoline when checking flow.*

Fuel tap O-ring (1), filter (2), and cup (3).

If the tap allows any gasoline to pass while in the "stop" position, the tap should be repaired or replaced, as gasoline may leak into the crankcase and dilute the oil.

Clean the filter screen and reinstall the cup and filter on the fuel tap. Use a new O-ring, if necessary. Do not overtighten the cup. Examine the fuel lines for leakage and for restriction caused by kinks or sharp bends. Check to see that the vent hole in the tank filler cap is not plugged, to preclude the possibility of fuel starvation.

FRONT SUSPENSION AND STEERING (6,000 mi/12 mo)

Steering Head Bearings

Precision steering and stable handling are very much dependent upon the steering head bearings. To check the bearings, place the bike on its center stand and swing the forks slowly through full steering travel. Movement should be smooth, light, and free from any binding. Check for play in the bearings by grabbing the bottom of the forks and trying to move them back and forth in line with the motorcycle. Play can be removed by tightening the steering head main nut. *Tighten no more than necessary to remove play.* If steering movement remains unsatisfactory the bearings should be replaced.

NOTE: *On machines equipped with a friction type steering damper, back the damper knob completely out when checking the steering. If the damper is operating unevenly or is binding, unbolt the damper components at the bottom of the steering stem and check the spring and plate for wear and damage.*

Fork Oil

The oil in the front forks should be changed regularly to ensure proper fork operation and extend seal life. Remove the small drain plug at the bottom of each fork leg and work the suspension until all the oil has been expelled. Replace the drain plugs. Remove the top filler plugs and fill each fork leg with the proper amount and grade of oil (see the specifications at the end of the chapter). After the oil has been poured into the forks, work them up and down slowly a few times to expel any air in the hydraulic passages before replacing the filler caps.

Front fork drain plug (1).

Fork top filler plugs (2).

REAR SUSPENSION (3,000 mi/6 mo)

Lubricate the swing arm pivot grease fitting(s) using a high-pressure grease gun. Wipe off any excess grease. There should be absolutely no side-play and the swing arm must not be bent or weakened from cracked welds, or else handling (especially at high speeds) will become erratic. Check that the bushings at the shock absorber mounting eyes are in good condition by attempting to move the swing arm up and down by hand and watching for play. Refer to the "Chassis" chapter.

Swing arm pivot grease fitting (1).

WHEELS, TIRES, and BRAKES (3,000 mi/6 mo)

Wheels

Check the tightness of the spokes, but unless a spoke is obviously too loose, do not attempt to tighten it or the wheel may become distorted. Tighten a loose spoke until it is approximately as taut as the neighboring spokes. If any spokes are broken or if a large number are loose, the wheel should be removed for complete servicing. Refer to chapter 8.

Check the runout of the wheel rim with a dial indicator if the tire is wearing unevenly or if a wobble is apparent at low speeds, growing progressively worse as speed is increased. If runout exceeds 0.08 in. (2 mm), the wheel must be trued or replaced.

Tires

Examine the tires for casing damage (splits, bubbles, etc.) and for objects lodged in the tread. Replace the tires before the tread is completely worn or when the tread is unevenly worn. Always maintain the correct air pressures.

Brakes

Brake lining wear on drum brakes can be determined by observing the angle formed by the brake operating lever and rod (at the brake drum) while the brake is applied. When the lever and rod move past perpendicular as the brake is applied, the brake shoes should be replaced.

Disc brake pad wear on the 450 can be determined by checking the clearance between the front of the caliper and the brake disc using a feeler gauge. Replace both pads when clearance is less than 0.08

Replace the disc pads on the 450K5 when either pad is worn to the red groove (4).

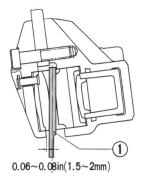

0.06~0.08in(1.5~2mm)

Replace disc pads on the 450K4 when clearance between the disc (1) and caliper is less than 0.08 in.

in. (2.0 mm). (On 1972 and later 450s, and the K5, replace both pads when either one has worn to the wear indicator groove.) Brake squeal can usually be eliminated by careful attention to pad alignment. Refer to chapter 8.

DISC BRAKE ADJUSTMENT

The disc brake is self-adjusting and is not provided with a means for manual adjustment to compensate for wear. If the brake lever feels spongy or lever travel is excessive, bleed the hydraulic system. Use only brake fluid conforming to SAE specification J1703. Refer to chapter 8.

DOUBLE LEADING SHOE FRONT BRAKE ADJUSTMENT

Adjustment can normally be made at the handlebar lever. Turn the adjuster until there is about 0.5–1.0 in. free-play at the lever. When adjustment at the lever is used up, further adjustment can be made at the bottom cable adjuster on the brake plate, after the locknut has been loosened. If both ends of the brake shoes are not contacting the drum at the same time (as evidenced by decreased braking efficiency and a spongy feel at the lever), loosen the locknut on the rod connecting the two brake arms and disconnect the rod from one of the brake arms. Turn the rod in the required direction to lengthen or shorten it to where both ends of the brake shoes are contacting the drum at the same time as the brake is applied. Retighten the locknut after the rod is connected at its correct length.

NOTE: *On the 450, it is not necessary to disconnect the rod. Since the rod is threaded on both ends, it can be rotated to change its working length once the locknuts are loosened. Note that one of the locknuts has a left-hand thread.*

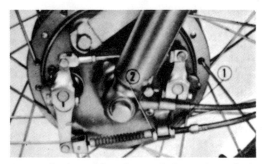

Bottom brake cable adjuster locknuts (1 and 2), and the brake arm connecting rod (arrow).

REAR BRAKE ADJUSTMENT

The brake should be adjusted so that there is approximately 1.0 in. (25 mm) free-play at the end of the pedal. Adjustment is made by turning the eccentric nut at the end of the operating rod. Make sure that the nut is seated properly on the lever and readjust the brake light switch if necessary.

Rear brake arm (1) and brake adjusting nut (2).

FINAL DRIVE

Chain Adjustment and Lubrication

To check chain adjustment, place the bike on the center stand and move the chain up and down at the midpoint of either run. If total movement exceeds 1.5 in., the chain is too loose and must be adjusted. The procedure is as follows:

1. Remove the rear axle nut cotter pin (if applicable), and loosen the nut until it can be turned by hand.

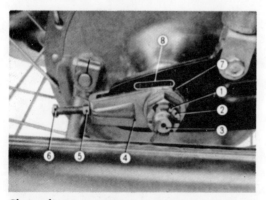

Chain adjuster components.

1. Cotter pin	5. Locknut
2. Axle nut	6. Adjusting bolt
3. Rear wheel axle	7. Index mark
4. Chain adjuster	8. Reference scale

2. Loosen the locknuts on the two chain adjuster bolts at the swing arm ends.

3. To tighten the chain, turn the adjuster bolts in equally until total chain slack is withing 1/2–3/4 in. Turning the adjusters an unequal amount will affect wheel alignment. Scales are provided on both sides of the swing arm to facilitiate adjustment. Make sure that they are both in the same position.

4. Tighten the adjuster bolt locknuts until they are just snug, while holding the bolts to keep them from turning. Do not overtighten.

5. Tighten the axle nut firmly and recheck chain movement. Do not forget to reinstall the cotter pin.

NOTE: *A dry chain should be lubricated before adjustment so that the links will not bind and restrict chain movement, making it seem tighter than it really is. If tension varies alternately between too loose and too tight as the chain is rotated, remove it and inspect for excessive wear after it has been cleaned.*

It is very important to keep the drive chain lubricated at all times. It will be necessary to use a special purpose motorcycle chain lubricant, as regular oil does not penetrate or cling adequately. Depending upon riding speed, mileage, weather, and chain and sprocket condition, it may be necessary to lubricate the chain as much as one or more times a day. To avoid excessive oil fling-off after the chain has been lubricated, allow the machine to sit for at least ten minutes before riding it. Most chain lubricants contain a thin compound to aid accurate delivery and complete penetration that will evaporate in a few minutes, leaving behind a thick lubricating compound that will not be thrown off.

A dry chain can cause a noticeable drop in performance and as much as a twenty-five percent increase in fuel consumption. And, of course, the risk of chain breakage is increased, which is never a pleasant occurrence. To prevent this, it is wise to replace the chain when it begins to give indications of becoming tired; i.e., stretching quickly after adjustment, tight and loose spots along the run, and being worn to a point where a link can be lifted more than about 1/4 in. away from the rear sprocket after adjustment. The chain is the weakest link in the drive train, and should be given the attention necessary to keep it in good condition.

Sprockets (3,000 mi / 6 mo)

Sprockets should be examined for wear. If the rear wheel is out of alignment, the sprocket teeth will show wear on their sides. If the sprocket is worn due to age or a worn chain, the teeth will be slightly hooked, with the hook facing away from the direction of rotation. If either sprocket is damaged or worn noticeably, both of the sprockets *and* the chain should be replaced. A worn sprocket can ruin a good chain, and, obviously, a worn chain can ruin a good sprocket. Sprocket life will also be reduced considerably by an improperly adjusted or unlubricated chain.

Storage Procedure

WINTER STORAGE

A few precautions should be taken when the motorcycle is to be out of use for a relatively short period of time, as during the winter season. If the following procedures are carried out, there will be very little likelihood of damage to the machine.

1. Wash the bike thoroughly and ride it until the engine is fully warmed up and all water has evaporated.

2. Change the engine oil.

3. Run the engine a minute or two to circulate the fresh engine oil.

4. Top up the fuel tank with the brand of gasoline normally used.

5. Turn off the fuel tap, remove the air filter element, and start the engine. Feed a few squirts of oil into each carburetor to thoroughly lubricate the valves, rings, and cylinders. Switch off the ignition and reinstall the filter element.

6. Remove the small plug from the bottom of each float bowl and allow them to drain.

CAUTION: *Do not allow fuel to spill onto the hot engine. Catch the gasoline in a small can or jar.*

7. Check the battery electrolyte level and state of charge. Recharge if low. Clean the battery and coat the terminals with petroleum jelly. Disconnect the positive cable from the battery during storage.

8. Lubricate all points on the machine: grease fittings, lever pivots, cables, chain, etc.

9. Apply a heavy coat of wax on all metal surfaces, taking special care with the chrome. If the wax is of the type that can be allowed to dry before polishing, it is not necessary to buff it before storage. Dust can later be easily removed by buffing the dry, unpolished wax.

10. Place the bike on its center stand and throw a protective cover over it. Make sure that the cover is made of a breathable material (an old blanket or piece of canvas will do), because a material such as plastic will encourage the formation of condensation on the inner surface.

When taking the bike out of storage, go over it completely, checking all points of maintenance (lubrication, battery charge, tightness of nuts and bolts, etc.) and engine tune. Reconnect the battery and check the oil level.

LONG TERM STORAGE

In addition to the winter storage procedures, a machine that is to be out of use for a period of time much longer than two months should be given the following attention.

Eliminate steps 4 and 7 above, and substitute:

4. Turn off the fuel tap, disconnect the fuel lines, and drain all but about one quart of gasoline from the tank. Pour half a cup of oil into the tank and rock the bike back and forth to coat the tank walls. Seal the fuel lines and fuel tap tubes.

7. Remove and fully charge the battery. It should be stored in a cool, dry environment and given a refresher charge every two months.

Periodic Maintenance Chart

EVERY 1,000 MILES/60 DAYS (SUMMER), 30 DAYS (WINTER):
Engine—
  1) Change oil.

EVERY 3,000 MILES/6 MONTHS:
Engine—
  1) Clean centrifugal oil filter.
  2) Service air filter element.
Clutch—
  1) Perform full clutch adjustment.

Periodic Maintenance Chart

EVERY 3,000 MILES/6 MONTHS:
Battery—
  1) Check electrolyte level and state of charge.
Fuel System—
  1) Clean fuel filter.
  2) Check fuel flow.
  3) Examine fuel lines and filler cap.
Rear Suspension—
  1) Lubricate swing arm pivot.
Wheels, Tires, and Brakes—
  1) Check tightness of spokes.
  2) Check wheel runout.
  3) Examine tires for wear and damage.
  4) Check brake wear.
Frame—
  1) Check tightness of nuts and bolts.
Final Drive—
  1) Service chain.
  2) Check sprockets for wear and damage.
EVERY 6,000 MILES/12 MONTHS:
Front Suspension and Steering—
  1) Check movement of steering head bearings.
  2) Change oil in fork legs.

EVERY 12,000 MILES/24 MONTHS:
Fuel System—
  1) Examine carburetor rubber caps.
Brakes—
  1) Examine the brake hoses and cylinders (CB 450K4 and K5).

Recommended Oils

	125	175	350	450
Engine Oil	10W-40 or 20W-50, service rating SE (formerly MS)			
capacity (pt)	2.5	3.2	4.2	6.0
Fork Oil	10W-30	10W-30	10W-30	10W-30
capacity (oz/cc)	4.9/140	①	②	③

① CB and CD 175—4.9/140; CL and SL 175—5.4/160
② CB and CL 350—6.75/200; SL 350—6.5/185
③ CB 450 through 1969, and CL 450—9.25/290; CB 450K4—7.2/225; CB 450K5—5.4/160

3 · Tune-Up

When performing a tune-up, you are restoring to peak efficiency certain engine components that are subject to changes in operating efficiency during use. A tune-up is nothing more than a series of adjustments performed in logical order, one at a time, to predetermined specifications. There is no guesswork involved. There are no complicated disassembly procedures and it is not necessary for you to have years of experience in diagnosing engine problems. All tune-up operations are quite straightforward.

A tune-up involves the following procedures, in the order shown:

1. Valve clearance adjustment.
2. Spark plug service or replacement and compression check.
3. Cam chain tensioner adjustment.
4. Ignition points service or replacement and ignition timing adjustment.
5. Carburetor synchronization and adjustment.

There are no special tools that are absolutely necessary to have when tuning up a twin cylinder Honda. All work can be completed with the tool kit that came with your bike, or preferably, using better quality tools of equivalent sizes. A test (continuity) light will be needed for ignition timing if you don't have a stroboscopic timing light. A test light is simply a 12-volt bulb with two wires attached so that it will light when connected to a power source. It can easily be made at home.

Bear in mind that items not covered in this chapter such as air and fuel filter servicing, cleaning and checking the battery, etc., can have an effect on the results of a tune-up. It is assumed that you have maintained your bike at least passably well. If not, refer to chapter 2 and carry out all engine-related maintenance procedures before beginning the tune-up.

Valve Clearance

Valves should be adjusted with the engine cold. Since the clearances you will be working with are relatively small, take care to adjust all valves as closely as possible to specification. Excessive clearance can cause unnecessary noise and accelerated cam lobe wear, and insufficient clearance can be responsible for hard starting, rough running, and ultimately, burned valves and valve seats. Take your time and make sure you've done it right. After the first or second time, you will develop a feel for valve clearance and the job will go much more easily and quickly.

ADJUSTMENT

125 and 175—All Models

1. Remove the circular alternator cover on the left side of the engine.

2. Unscrew the four adjuster access caps on the cylinder head.

3. Remove the spark plugs.

4. Turn the crankshaft in the normal direction of rotation until the "T" mark on the alternator rotor lines up with the timing index mark.

The timing index mark (1) and the "T" mark (2) must be aligned.

5. Both pistons will be at top dead center (TDC) of the stroke, however, one piston will be on the compression stroke and the other will be on the exhaust stroke. To determine which piston is on compression, check to see which pair of valves (intake and exhaust) are fully closed, in which case there will be clearance at both rocker arms. The valves for the piston that is on compression are correctly positioned for adjustment.

6. Check the clearance between the rocker arm and valve stem for the two valves using the appropriate feeler gauge. Correct clearance is 0.002 in. (0.05 mm) for both valves.

7. If adjustment is necessary, loosen the adjuster screw locknut and turn the screw in the required direction until the feeler gauge fits with some resistance. Tighten the locknut while holding the adjuster from turning, and recheck clearance.

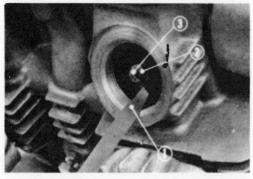

A feeler gauge (1) is used to check valve clearance, as shown. Adjustment is made by loosening the locknut (2) and turning the adjuster screw (3).

8. When both valves are correctly adjusted, rotate the crankshaft through one complete turn (360°) and align the "T" mark with the index mark again. The other piston is now on compression and its two valves are correctly positioned for adjustment. Repeat steps 6 and 7.

350—All Models

1. Remove the alternator rotor cover on the left side of the engine.

2. Remove the ignition points cover and the small matching cover on the right side.

3. Remove the four valve access caps on the cylinder head.

NOTE: *Access to the valves is made easier if the fuel tank is removed, but this is not absolutely essential.*

4. Remove the spark plugs.

5. Rotate the crankshaft in the normal direction of rotation while observing the left intake (rear) valve spring and rocker arm. When the valve spring is fully compressed and then starts to return, turn the crankshaft slowly in the same direction until the "LT" mark on the alternator rotor and the timing index mark are aligned. At this point, the left piston is at top dead center (TDC) of its compression stroke and both the intake and exhaust valves on that side should be fully closed (clearance at both rocker arms).

To adjust the valves on the left cylinder, the timing index mark (1) must be aligned with the "LT" mark on the alternator rotor (2), and the left piston must be on its compression stroke (clearance at both valves).

6. Check the clearance between the rocker arm and valve stem on the two left-side valves using the appropriate feeler gauges. Correct clearance is 0.002 in. (0.05 mm) for the intake valve, and 0.004 in. (0.1 mm) for the exhaust valve.

7. Adjustment is made by rotating the eccentric rocker arm shafts. If adjustment is necessary, loosen the appropriate adjus-

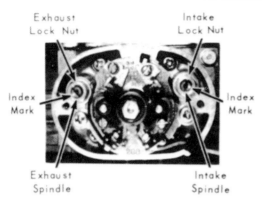

The left-side valve adjuster screws are located under the ignition points cover.

Check valve clearance using a feeler gauge (1). If adjustment is necessary, loosen the locknut (3) and turn the adjusting screw (2) in the required direction.

To adjust the right-side valves, the timing index mark (1) must be aligned with the "T" mark (2), and the right piston must be on its compression stroke (clearance at both valves).

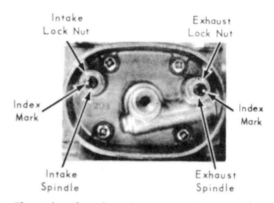

The right-side valve adjusters are located under the small chrome cover on the cylinder head.

ter locknut located next to the ignition points base plate, and turn the adjuster in the required direction until the feeler gauge fits with some resistance. Tighten the locknut while holding the adjuster from turning, and recheck clearance.

NOTE: *The small index mark on the end of each adjuster must be pointed outwards (away from the center of the cylinder head) for the valve rocker arms to operate properly. If the mark is pointing inward, rotate the adjuster about ½ turn so that the mark points outward and reset the valve clearance.*

8. When both left-side valves are correctly adjusted, rotate the crankshaft 180° (½ turn) in the normal direction of rotation to align the "T" mark on the alternator rotor with the timing index mark. The right-side piston is now on compression and its two valves are correctly positioned for adjustment. Repeat steps 6 and 7 for the right-side valves. The adjusters are located under the small chrome cover on the right side.

450—All Models

1. Remove the fuel tank.

2. Unbolt and remove the front and rear cylinder head covers.

3. Remove the ignition points cover and the alternator rotor cover.

4. Remove the spark plugs.

5. Rotate the crankshaft slowly in the normal direction of rotation and observe the left-side cam followers. When the followers have travelled downward fully and start to rise, turn the crankshaft slowly until the "LT" mark on the alternator rotor and the timing index mark are aligned. At this point, the left piston is at top dead center (TDC) of its compression stroke and both the intake and exhaust valves on that side should be fully closed (clearance between the camshaft and cam followers).

6. Check the clearance between the camshaft and cam follower on the two left-side valves using the appropriate feeler gauge. Correct clearance is 0.002 in. for both valves.

7. Adjustment is made by rotating the

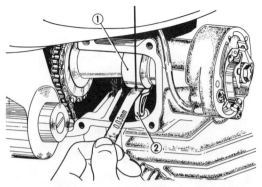

To adjust the valves on the left cylinder the timing index mark (1) must be aligned with the "LT" mark on the alternator rotor (2), and the left piston must be on its compression stroke (clearance at both valves).

As can be seen, valve clearance is measured between the camshaft lobe (1) and the cam follower (2).

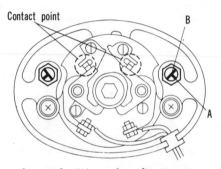

Check valve clearance with a feeler gauge (1). If adjustment is necessary, loosen the locknut and turn the adjusting screw. All adjusting screws are accessible from the outside of the engine except for the left cylinder exhaust valve adjuster (2), which is located under the ignition points cover as shown.

The index marks (A) on the adjusting screws (B) must be pointing away from the center of the cylinder head.

eccentric cam follower shafts. If adjustment is necessary, loosen the appropriate adjuster locknut and turn the adjuster in the required direction until the feeler gauge fits with some resistance. Tighten the locknut while holding the adjuster from turning, and recheck clearance. (The left-side exhaust valve adjuster is located next to the ignition points base plate.)

NOTE: *The small index mark on the end of each adjuster must be pointed outward (away from the center of the cylinder head) for the cam followers to operate properly. If the mark is pointing inward, rotate the adjuster about ½ turn so that the mark points outward and reset the valve clearance.*

8. When both left-side valves are correctly adjusted, rotate the crankshaft 180°

(½ turn) in the normal direction of rotation to align the "T" mark on the alternator rotor with the timing index mark. (On early models with a four-speed transmission, rotate the crankshaft one full turn.) The right-side piston is now on compression and its two valves are correctly positioned for adjustment. Repeat steps 6 and 7 for the right-side valves.

Spark Plug Service and Compression Check

SPARK PLUGS

The condition of the spark plugs has a great deal of influence upon how the engine runs. Regardless of what they look like, spark plugs with many thousands of miles on them should be replaced as a matter of course at this time. The spark plug wires and connectors should also be checked. Replace any component that does not appear to be in perfect condition. The ignition coils should be capable of producing a fat, hot spark to fire the spark plugs properly.

Examine the tips of the plugs for any of the conditions shown in the chart. Check also for cracked insulators and damaged threads.

Light carbon deposits can be removed in a spark plug cleaning machine (most garages will do it for a small charge), or by using a small, sharp instrument to scrape it off. Heavy carbon deposits are indicative of either a rich fuel mixture or a cold spark plug heat range. Be wary, however, of using a hotter plug unless actual plug fouling is occurring. Heat range does not refer to spark intensity, but to the ability of a spark plug to dissipate heat. A cold plug will dissipate heat rapidly, while a hotter plug will dissipate heat more slowly. The danger in using too hot a plug is that it will retain enough heat to cause pre-ignition and eventually severe over-

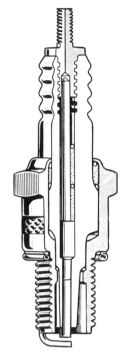
Spark plug construction.

Spark plug condition

Electrode coated with carbon deposit

Electrode fouled with oil

Electrode overheated or burnt

heating and piston failure. Generally, you should either continue using the standard heat range as recommended by the manufacturer, or select the coldest heat range that it is possible to use without fouling.

Oil fouling indicates excessive oil consumption, caused by worn or sticking piston rings, worn valve stems and guides, or faulty valve stem oil seals. Do not attempt to cure oil fouling by using spark plugs of a hotter heat range. The cause of oil burning should be determined and corrected. Run a compression check as indicated in the next section.

Burnt electrodes indicate too lean a fuel mixture or too hot a spark plug heat range. Check for air leaks at the carburetors and intake tubes, and check the fuel tap and lines for restrictions. Try using a set of plugs one step colder in heat range.

Replace spark plugs that have damaged insulators or threads. It is a good idea, in any case, to replace both plugs at the same time. If the old plugs are to be reused, clean the threads and insulators thoroughly before installing. Gap the electrodes to about 0.025 in. and lubricate the threads before installing either old or new spark plugs, and tighten them to 12–15 ft lbs in the cylinder head. The threads in

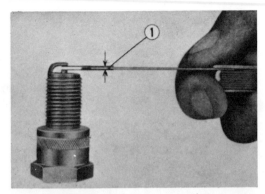

Check spark plug gap (1) using a feeler gauge. Adjust gap to about 0.025 in. by bending the outer electrode.

the aluminum cylinder head can be cross-threaded or stripped quite easily and great care should be exercised when starting the plugs into the threads and tightening them. The plugs should not be under-tightened, however, as a loose plug cannot dissipate heat efficiently and will overheat. Do not install the plugs until a compression check has been run.

COMPRESSION CHECK

A compression check will tell you whether or not you have trouble in the top end. Compression pressure in each cylinder should be above 140 psi, and the variation between cylinders should not exceed 15 psi. To obtain accurate readings, make sure that the compression gauge is properly seated in the spark plug hole and hold the throttle fully open while cranking the engine until the needle on the gauge stops advancing. Low readings can indicate a leaking head gasket, valves that are adjusted too tightly or burnt, or worn piston rings.

If you obtain low readings, use an oil can to squirt a shot or two of engine oil into each cylinder, in turn, and recheck compression pressure. If the pressure increases significantly, the indication is that the rings are worn. If it does not increase and both cylinders are low or there is evidence of a leak at the cylinder head joint, chances are that the head gasket is blown. If there is no evidence of a bad head gasket or worn rings, it is probable that the valves are causing low compression. To make certain that it is not merely insufficient valve clearance that is doing you in, back off the valve adjusters on the offending cylinder(s) to increase clearance and recheck compression. Do this even if you have just adjusted the valves, because you may have goofed. If you *still* don't have good compression, button it up and make a date for a top end overhaul, because a tune-up is not going to help you at this point. Be sure to reset the valves you loosened if you plan on riding in the meantime.

Cam Chain Adjustment

125 AND 175—ALL MODELS

1. Remove the alternator rotor cover.
2. Remove the left-side intake valve access cap.
3. Turn the alternator rotor clockwise (the opposite direction of normal rotation) until the left intake valve opens fully (spring compressed) and begins to close.
4. Turn the alternator rotor counterclockwise until the left intake valve barely moves.

Measuring compression pressure with a compression gauge (1).

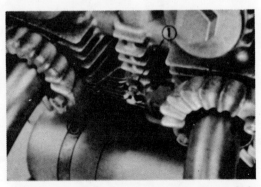

Cam chain tensioner locknut (1) and adjuster bolt (2).

5. Loosen the cam chain adjuster locknut and back the adjuster bolt out a few turns to free the tensioner. The tensioner will automatically take up the chain slack. Retighten the adjuster bolt and locknut.

350—ALL MODELS

1. Remove the alternator cover.
2. Remove the two left cylinder valve access caps.
3. Turn the alternator rotor slowly in the normal direction of rotation until the "LT" mark lines up with the timing index mark. The left piston is now at TDC.
4. Check to see if the left-side tappets are free. If they are, the left piston is on the compression stroke. If not, rotate the engine 360° (one full turn) in the normal direction of rotation and realign the marks. The left piston should be at TDC of its compression stroke.

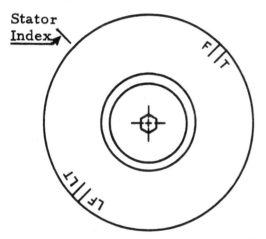

Stator
Index

The engine is properly set up for cam chain adjustment when the left piston is 90° past TDC of its compression stroke, as indicated by the action of the valves and the position of the alternator rotor marks. Refer to the text.

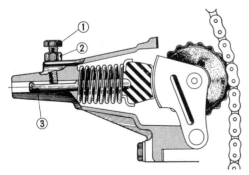

A cross-section of the tensioner assembly, located at the rear of the cylinder barrel. Shown is the adjuster bolt (1), locknut (2), and the tensioner guide rod (3).

5. Now, turn the alternator rotor counterclockwise about 90° (¼ turn after the "LT" mark). The engine is properly set up for adjustment of the cam chain at this point. Loosen the locknut and the adjuster bolt, and the cam chain slack will be taken up automatically by the tensioner. Retighten the adjuster bolt and locknut.

450—5-SPEED MODELS

1. Remove the gas tank.
2. Unbolt and remove the front and rear cylinder head covers.
3. Remove the alternator cover.
4. Rotate the crankshaft slowly in the normal direction of rotation and observe the left-side cam followers. When the followers have traveled downward fully and start to rise, turn the crankshaft until the "LT" mark on the alternator rotor and the timing index mark are aligned. At this point, the left piston is at TDC of its compression stroke and both the intake and exhaust valves on that side should be fully closed (clearance between the camshaft and cam followers).
5. Now, turn the alternator rotor counterclockwise about 90° (¼ turn after the "LT" mark). The engine is properly set up for adjustment of the cam chain at this point. Loosen the locknut and the adjuster bolt, and the cam chain slack will be taken up automatically by the tensioner. Retighten the adjuster bolt and locknut.

450—4 SPEED MODELS

Follow steps 1, 2, 3, 4, and 6 in the preceding section on five-speed models, omitting step 5. The crankshaft is correctly positioned for cam chain adjustment when the left piston is at TDC of its compression stroke.

ALTERNATE PROCEDURE—350 AND 450

If you can't obtain satisfactory cam chain adjustment using the previously described methods, try adjusting the tensioner in the following manner:

Loosen the locknut and adjuster bolt. Insert a thin instrument such as a stiff piece of wire or a small screwdriver into the tail section of the tensioner and seat it gently against the end of the tensioner rod inside. (On early 450s, the tensioner rod protrudes from the tail section.) Now, turn the engine over slowly; you can feel the rod move back and forth as the cam chain slack varies. Do this several times and take note of the point at which the rod is farthest in (closest to the engine). Continue turning the engine over slowly until you succeed in stopping it at this point. *Do not use pressure to force the tensioner rod in.* When this is accomplished, the cam chain slack is on the tensioner side of the engine and the tensioner has automatically moved in to take up slack. Tighten the adjuster bolt and locknut to lock the tensioner in this position.

This method has been used for many years and is quite effective if carried out carefully. If you do not use pressure to force the rod in, there is no danger of the cam chain being overtight.

Ignition Points and Ignition Timing

IGNITION POINTS SERVICE— ALL MODELS

Inspection, Cleaning, and Replacement

Examine the contact points for pitting, misalignment, and excessive wear of the rubbing block that rides on the breaker cam. If the points are in good condition except for a slight amount of pitting, they may be cleaned up using an ignition points file. Allow the points to spring shut on the file and move the file back and forth without exerting any extra pressure against the points surface. Remove dirt

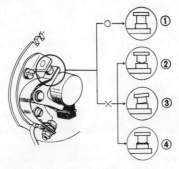

Various conditions of the ignition points.

1. Points properly aligned and in good condition
2. Worn or burnt contact surfaces
3. Misalignment
4. Contamination of contact surfaces

and grit from between the points by pulling a thick piece of paper, such as a business card, through the points two or three times.

If the points are heavily pitted, replace the points and condenser(s). The components can be unscrewed and removed from the base plate after the electrical leads have been disconnected. Make sure that any insulating washers are replaced in their original positions when reconnecting the wires. Place a drop or two of gasoline or other non-oily solvent on a piece of paper and pull it through the points to remove any dirt or preservative coating on the contact surfaces. Put a *small* dab of distributor cam lubricant or other high-melting-point grease on the contact breaker cam. This will prevent the points rubbing block from wearing excessively and reducing point gap.

Adjustment—125 and 175

Adjust the point gap by loosening the securing screws and swivelling the stationary contact point toward or away from the moving contact as required. The breaker cam must be positioned where it will give maximum point opening. The gap should be set at 0.012–0.016 in. The gap is not particularly critical, as long as it is within the specified range.

The contact breaker arm (1) and the breaker points (2). The point gap can be adjusted by loosening the two screws (arrows) and repositioning the stationary contact.

Adjustment—350 and 450

Point gap should be adjusted to 0.012–0.016 in. Adjust one set at a time by loosening the securing screws and swivelling the stationary contact point toward or away from the moving contact as required. The cam must be positioned where it will give maximum opening for the set of points being adjusted. The point gap is not particularly critical as long as it is within the specified range. However, you should try to adjust each set of points so that their gaps are as close to identical as possible.

Loosen the securing screws (1) for one point set at a time and adjust the points gap (2) by repositioning the stationary contact.

IGNITION TIMING

There are two methods of accurately determining and resetting ignition timing. The easiest way, commonly referred to as the static (engine not running) timing method, requires no special equipment other than a small 12-volt bulb with two leads connected to it. Static timing is quite satisfactory if carried out carefully. The second method, known as dynamic (engine running) timing, requires the use of a stroboscopic ignition timing light. The advantage of using this method is that it checks ignition timing while the ignition advance unit is in operation, taking into account any slight variations in advance characteristics that stem from unavoidable manufacturing tolerances. Also, any ignition advance defects will show up clearly under a strobe light. If you own or have access to a stroboscopic timing light, use it. If not, use the static timing method and don't worry about it.

Static Timing Procedure—125 and 175

1. Connect one of the test light leads to the small bolt that fastens the electrical supply wire to the point set. Ground the other test light lead on the engine.
2. Switch the ignition on and turn the engine in the normal direction of rotation until the "F" mark on the alternator rotor is aligned with the timing index mark.
3. The test light should light at the

Connect the test light lead to the terminal shown (arrow). The timing can be altered by rotating the base plate after the securing screws (3) have been loosened.

Timing index mark (1) and the "F" mark on the alternator rotor (2).

same instant the marks are aligned. If not, loosen the points base plate securing screws and rotate the base plate in the required direction until the light just comes on as the timing marks are aligned. Retighten the securing screws. Both cylinders are now correctly timed.

Static Timing Procedure—350 and 450

1. Make sure that the point gaps are as close to identical as possible.
2. Connect one of the test light leads to the small bolt that fastens the electrical supply wire to the left (L) point set. Ground the other test light lead on the engine.
3. Switch the ignition on and turn the

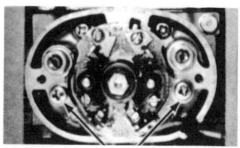

The timing can be adjusted after the base plate securing screws have been loosened.

The timing index mark (1) and the "LF" (left cylinder firing) mark on the alternator rotor.

engine in the normal direction of rotation until the "LF" mark on the alternator rotor aligns with the timing index mark.

4. The test light should light at the same instant the marks are aligned. If not, loosen the points base plate securing screws and rotate the base plate in the required direction until the light just comes on as the timing marks are aligned. Retighten the securing screws. The left cylinder is now correctly timed.

5. If the point gaps are the same, the right cylinder should also be correctly timed at this point. To check this, transfer the test light lead to the right (R) point set. Turn the alternator rotor counterclockwise 180° (½ turn) until the "F" mark aligns with the timing index mark. If adjustment is necessary, loosen the securing

The timing index mark (1) and the "F" (right cylinder firing) mark.

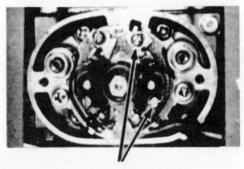

Right cylinder point set securing screws.

screws on the right point set and alter the point gap until the light comes on as the marks are aligned. Retighten the screws and double-check the timing on both cylinders. Make sure that point gap is still within 0.012–0.016 in.

Dynamic Timing Procedure—125 and 175

1. Connect the strobe light as per manufacturer's instructions, picking up the impulses from either cylinder.

2. Start the engine and adjust the idle, if necessary, to the recommended speed. (Refer to the specifications at the end of the chapter.)

3. Aim the light at the timing marks. At idle speed the "F" mark should be aligned with the timing index mark. If not, loosen the points base plate securing screws and rotate the base plate in the required direction until the marks are aligned. Retighten the screws.

4. To check the timing at full ignition advance, increase the engine speed to approximately 2,000 rpm (175) or 4,000 rpm (125) and hold it steady. The timing index mark should be between the two marks on the alternator rotor that are about 35° to the left of the "F" and "T" marks. If it is, both cylinders are correctly timed and the ignition advance unit is functioning properly.

Timing index mark (1), "F" (firing) mark used for static timing (2), and the full advance marks (3) used for dynamic timing.

5. If it is not, or if the timing is unsteady even though the engine speed is held constant, the fault probably lies with either the ignition points or the advance unit springs (assuming that the timing is correct at idle speed). To examine the advance unit, first scribe a line on the contact breaker plate and cylinder head to facilitate correct reassembly, then take out the two screws and remove the breaker plate assembly. The advance unit can be

The ignition advance unit.

removed, if necessary, after the mounting bolt is unscrewed. Look for weak or broken springs, and stiff governor weight pivots. When installing the advance unit, make sure that the camshaft oil seal is in good condition, and that the pin in the camshaft is properly located in the groove in the advance unit.

Dynamic Timing Procedure— 350 and 450

1. Make sure that the point gaps are as close to identical as possible.
2. Connect the strobe light as per manufacturer's instructions, picking up the impulses from the left cylinder.
3. Start the engine and adjust the idle, if necessary, to the recommended speed. (Refer to the specifications at the end of the chapter.)
4. Aim the light at the timing marks. At idle speed the "LF" mark should be aligned with the timing index mark. If not, loosen the points base plate securing screws and rotate the base plate in the required direction until the marks are aligned. Retighten the screws.
5. To check the timing at full ignition advance, increase the engine speed to approximately 3,500 rpm and hold it steady. The timing index mark should be between

The timing index mark (1), "LF" (left cylinder firing) mark used for static timing (2), and the full advance marks (3) used for dynamic timing.

the two advance marks on the alternator rotor. If it is, the left cylinder is correctly timed. If it is not, or if the timing is unsteady even though the engine speed is held constant, the fault probably lies with the ignition points or the advance unit springs (see step 7).

6. To time the right cylinder, shut the engine off, transfer the strobe light lead to the right cylinder, and restart the engine. If the "F" mark and timing index mark are not aligned at normal idling speed, loosen the screws securing the right point set and alter the point gap until the marks align. Check the timing at full ignition advance in the same manner as for the left cylinder in step 5, above. Make sure that point gap is still within 0.012–0.016 in.

The timing index mark (1) and right cylinder firing mark (2), and the full advance marks (3).

7. If the timing is unsteady as the advance unit comes into operation, scribe a line on the contact breaker plate and cylinder head and remove the breaker plate assembly. The advance unit can be removed, if necessary, after the retaining bolt is unscrewed. Look for weak or broken springs, and stiff governor weight pivots. When reinstalling the advance unit, make sure that the pin in the camshaft is properly located in the groove at the back of the unit.

The ignition advance unit.

Carburetor Adjustments

Carburetor tuning is largely a matter of patience and feel, the latter being developed with practice. Take your time and work with the procedures until you feel confident that the bike is responding properly. Do not hesistate to check and re-check your settings until you know they are right. After you have done it a few times, you will be able to tune the carburetors quite rapidly and accurately.

TWIN CARBURETOR SYNCHRONIZATION

CB / CL 350, SL 350 (1970 only), and CB / CL 450

Synchronizing the constant velocity carburetors used on the larger Honda twins can be accomplished quite easily. The idea is to adjust the throttle cables so that the throttles open at the same time and by the same amount as the throttle grip is turned. Place your hand under the carburetors and note the movement of the throttle levers as the throttle is opened. If adjustment is required, loosen the locknut and turn the cable adjuster in the required direction until both throttle slides open at the same time.

Left carburetor throttle cable adjuster (1) and locknut (2), 350 shown.

CB / CL 125 and 175, SL 350K1 and K2

To synchronize the throttle slides on these models it will be necessary, first, to remove the air filter(s) or air filter tubes so that the slides are accessible. Place a finger into each of the carburetor bores so that you are lightly touching the slides

and slowly open the throttle grip a small amount. Both slides should start to rise at the same time. If they do not, raise the rubber boot on top of either carburetor and loosen the adjuster locknut. Turn the adjuster in the required direction until the slides are synchronized. If both slides are rising and falling at the same time a single click (rather than two separate clicks) should be heard as the throttle grip is released and the slides hit bottom.

IDLE ADJUSTMENT— ALL MODELS

1. Back off the throttle cable adjuster at the handlebar to provide about ¼ in. of slack in the cable.
2. Start the engine and adjust the idle (after it has warmed up) to the recommended speed with the throttle stop screw(s). Refer to the specifications at the end of the chapter.
3. Turn the air screw(s) slowly in or out to obtain the highest idle speed consistent with smoothness. Standard air screw opening is approximately one turn from full open, and it should not be necessary to ex-

Throttle stop screw (1) and air screw (2), all models except CB/CL 350, CB/CL 450, and SS 125.

Throttle stop screw (1) and air screw (2), CB/CL 350 and SS 125.

Air screw (1) and throttle stop screw (2), all 450 models.

ceed ¼ turn in either direction from this setting.

4. Check for even firing of the cylinders by feeling the exhaust pressure with your hand. Reset the throttle stop screws again, if necessary, to obtain the correct idle speed.

NOTE: *If the carburetors are unresponsive to large changes in air screw openings, investigate the following possible causes: clogged air passage, worn air screw, float level too high, or loose low*

speed jet. If the air screw adjustment requires less than ½ turn opening, look for: clogged low speed jet or jet passage, float level too low, or worn air screw seat.

5. Adjust the throttle cable play to the desired amount at the adjuster near the throttle grip. Swing the handlebars to full lock in both directions to make sure that the throttle cable is not binding and pulling the carburetors open.

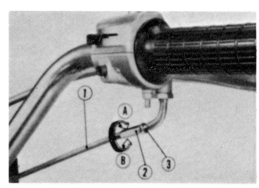

Throttle cable (1), cable adjuster (2), and adjuster locknut (3). Turning the adjuster in direction A decreases cable play, and turning in direction B increases play.

Tune-Up Specifications

	125	175	350	450
VALVE CLEARANCE (cold)				
Intake: (in./mm)	0.002/0.05	0.002/0.05	0.002/0.05	0.002/0.05
Exhaust: (in./mm)	0.002/0.05	0.002/0.05	0.004/0.1	0.002/0.05
COMPRESSION				
Pressure (psi)	140 (115–170)	140 (115–170)	170 (145–200)	185 (160–210)
Maximum Variation (psi) *	15	15	15	15
IGNITION				
Spark Plugs:				
standard make **	NGK	NGK	NGK	NGK
type	D8HS	D8HS	B8ES or B9E	B8ES or B9E
gap (in.)	0.025–0.028	0.025–0.028	0.025–0.028	0.025–0.028
Point Gap (in.)	0.012–0.016	0.012–0.016	0.012–0.016	0.012–0.016
CARBURETION				
Idle Speed (rpm)	①	①	1,000–1,300	1,000–1,200
Air Screw Opening	1⅛ ± ¼	1⅛ ± ¼	②	1.0 ±¼

* Between cylinders.
** Other reputable makes are also acceptable. Be sure to select plugs of the correct heat range, reach, and diameter. Most spark plug application charts also have conversion tables and a heat range chart, enabling you to select the spark plug that fits your needs exactly.
① Single carburetor models—1,000; twin carburetor models 1,200
② CB/CL 350 and 1970 SL 350—¾ ± ⅛; SL 350K1 and K2—1 ± ¼

Spark Plug Size and
Heat Range Chart

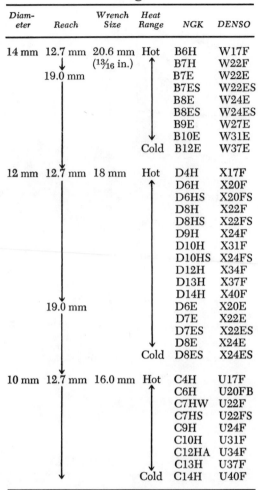

Diameter	Reach	Wrench Size	Heat Range	NGK	DENSO
14 mm	12.7 mm ↓ 19.0 mm	20.6 mm (13⁄16 in.)	Hot ↑	B6H	W17F
				B7H	W22F
				B7E	W22E
				B7ES	W22ES
				B8E	W24E
				B8ES	W24ES
				B9E	W27E
			↓	B10E	W31E
			Cold	B12E	W37E
12 mm	12.7 mm	18 mm	Hot ↑	D4H	X17F
				D6H	X20F
				D6HS	X20FS
				D8H	X22F
				D8HS	X22FS
				D9H	X24F
				D10H	X31F
				D10HS	X24FS
				D12H	X34F
				D13H	X37F
				D14H	X40F
	19.0 mm			D6E	X20E
				D7E	X22E
				D7ES	X22ES
				D8E	X24E
			Cold	D8ES	X24ES
10 mm	12.7 mm	16.0 mm	Hot ↑	C4H	U17F
				C6H	U20FB
				C7HW	U22F
				C7HS	U22FS
				C9H	U24F
				C10H	U31F
				C12HA	U34F
			↓	C13H	U37F
			Cold	C14H	U40F

4 · Engine and Transmission

When preparing to do any work on the engine it is essential that cleanliness is maintained and that an area suitable to work in is available. Naturally, the tools and parts necessary to accomplish the task are also required. It is best, when performing a job for the first time, to familiarize yourself as much as possible with the components and procedures you will be working with. The time spent here will be well rewarded through an increase in knowledge and confidence, and a decrease in needless mistakes and aggravation. In addition, the satisfaction gained in knowing that the job was done right is immeasurable.

Cleanliness and careful approach are imperative! A quick ring job could become a complete engine disassembly if simple precautions are not taken. Lay out and mark all parts in sequence as they are being removed; this way the correct order of reassembly will be obvious. If possible, clean the engine parts in solvent and blow them dry with compressed air. When cleaning ball or roller bearings, don't spin them until they have been thoroughly cleaned and dried because particles in the solvent bath often get caught in the bearing races and can only be removed with high pressure air.

A good general rule to follow when disassembling an unfamiliar engine is to restrain yourself. When a nut or bolt seems to require an inordinate amount of pres-

sure to remove it, don't just give it the old heave-ho effort. Instead; sit back, relax for a few minutes, and then survey the situation. More engine damage is caused by swinging a heavy wrench than most other causes combined, and the reason is usually a mechanic who is blinded with frustration. These engines are made primarily with aluminum alloy, so you have to be careful.

With proper care and decent treatment, your engine can be made to run as well, or better than, new.

125 and 175 Models

*ENGINE REMOVAL AND
INSTALLATION*

1. Remove the footpeg, kick-start pedal, and shift lever. Drain the engine oil.
2. Remove the entire exhaust system from each side as a unit.
3. Disconnect the wires from the spark plugs and tuck them up out of the way.
4. Remove the small cover from the right side of the cylinder head and disconnect the tachometer cable from the tachometer drive.
5. Remove the seat.
6. Turn off the fuel tap and disconnect the fuel lines from the carburetors.

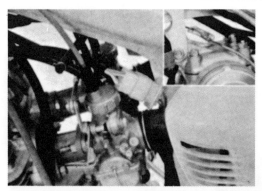

Disconnecting the electrical leads.

7. Uncouple the electrical leads at the connectors. Refer to the accompanying illustration.

8. Loosen the air filter tube clamps.

9. Unscrew the carburetor caps and withdraw the slides. Tie them out of the way. (Simply disconnect the cable from the carburetor on the CD 125.)

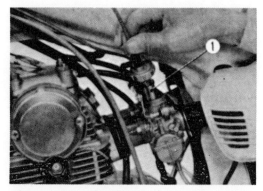

Removing the carburetor slides.

10. Remove the left-side rear crankcase cover. Separate the drive chain at the master link and disconnect the clutch cable from the release lever.

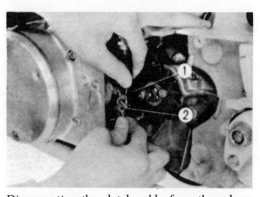

Disconnecting the clutch cable from the release lever.

11. Disconnect the starter motor cable from the starter solenoid (if applicable).

12. Take out the nine engine mounting bolts and remove the engine from the right side.

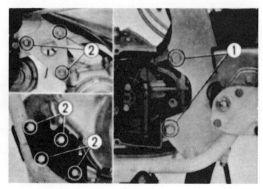

Engine mounting bolts.

Installation is a reversal of the removal procedure. Note the following points:

1. Do not forget to connect the battery ground cable when installing the engine mounting bolts.

2. The chain master link clip should be installed so that the closed end faces the direction of forward rotation.

3. Make sure that the steel ball has been installed in the clutch release lever before reinstalling the crankcase cover.

4. Do not forget to refill the engine with oil.

TOP END OVERHAUL

Cylinder Head Removal

1. Remove the engine from the frame.

2. Unscrew the cylinder head nuts and then the head nut (175 only). Remove the cam cover.

3. Rotate the crankshaft until the cam chain master link is accessible, then dis-

Cylinder head nuts, 125.

Cylinder head nuts and bolt (1), 175.

connect the cam chain. Attach a length of wire to each end of the chain so that it will not fall into the crankcase.

4. Lift the head carefully off of the cylinder barrel.

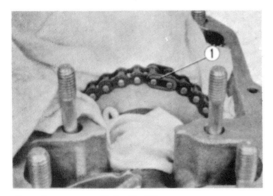

Cam chain master link clip (1).

Cylinder Barrel and Piston Removal

1. Unscrew the cylinder retaining bolt(s) and carefully lift the cylinder off of the crankcase. Take care to prevent the pistons from being damaged on the studs as the cylinder is withdrawn over them.

The cylinder can be removed after the retaining bolt (1) has been unscrewed.

2. Remove the wrist pin circlips from the pistons.

CAUTION: *Do not allow the circlips to fall into the crankcase. To avoid having to split the cases to retrieve a clip, cover the crankcase opening with a cloth.*

3. Remove the wrist pins from the pistons. Mark the pistons, inside the skirt, so that they can be reinstalled in their original positions.

Component Inspection and Service

CAMSHAFT

The camshaft can be removed, if necessary, after the following components have been removed: left and right head side covers, ignition points breaker plate assembly, ignition advance unit (located under the breaker plate), and the valve adjuster access caps. Rotate the camshaft until the rocker arms are resting on the heel of the cam, and remove the rocker arm shafts and rocker arms. (On the 125 it will be necessary to remove the rocker shaft end plate.) Lift the camshaft out of

Take off the cover (1) and remove the points breaker plate assembly (2).

Hold the camshaft from turning with a block of wood (1) and unscrew the ignition advance unit securing bolt (2).

Take out the screws and remove the side covers (1).

Remove the rocker arm shaft end plate (125 only).

1. Rocker shaft end plate
2. Plate retaining bolt
3. Rocker arm shafts

the cylinder head. Using a micrometer, measure the camshaft end diameters, cam height, and cam base circle diameter. Compare your results with the specifications at the end of the chapter. Replace the camshaft if the measurements are outside the serviceable limit, or if the cam lobes are scored or worn.

Slide the rocker shafts out (2) and remove the rocker arms (1).

VALVE ROCKER ASSEMBLY

Measure the diameter of the rocker arm bores and rocker arm shafts and compare

with the specifications. Check that the rocker arm pads that contact the camshaft lobes are not excessively worn. Check the cam chain for stretch and replace it if necessary.

CYLINDER HEAD AND VALVES

Compress the springs (Honda spring compressor no. 07031-21601) and remove the collars, retainers, springs, and valves. Check the following measurements against the specifications at the end of the chapter: valve length, stem diameter, head thickness, valve face concentricity, and valve spring free length. Replace valves as necessary. When replacing worn valves it is wise also, to replace the valve guides, which can be driven out of the head with a suitably sized drift. Since the guides are an interference fit, oversize guides should be used.

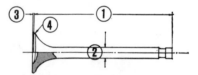

Valve measurements.

1. Length
2. Stem diameter
3. Head thickness
4. Valve face concentricity (out of round)

If the valve seat is burnt, worn, or damaged in any way, it should be recut. Valve seat angle is 45°. Seat width should not be greater than 0.08 in. (2 mm). Nominal seat width is 0.04 in. (0.1 mm).

NOTE: *Do not attempt to reface the valves or refinish the valve stem ends, as these surfaces have a thin stellite facing that will be destroyed if cut.*

Carefully scrape carbon deposits from the combustion chambers and thoroughly clean the cylinder head. Before the valves are installed, whether they are the original ones or new, they should be lapped into their seats so that a perfect seal will be obtained. To properly lap a valve, first place three small dabs of lapping compound around the valve face. Insert the valve into the guide and, using a lapping tool (available at most auto supply stores), rotate the valve back and forth lightly by rotating the handle of the lapping tool between the palms of your hands. Reposition the valve every few seconds and examine the valve face and seat surfaces. When they have be-

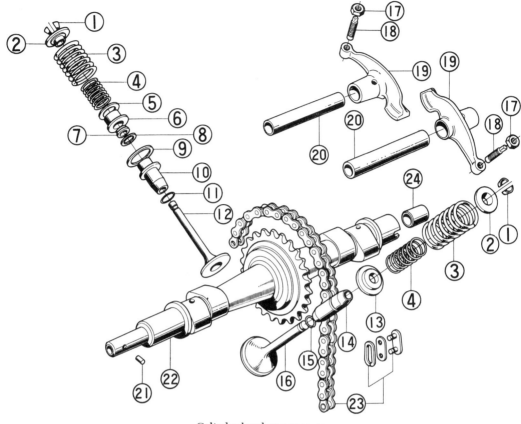

Cylinder head components.

1. Valve collar	9. Valve spring seat B	17. Valve tappet adjusting locknut
2. Valve retainer	10. Exhaust valve guide	18. Valve tappet adjuster
3. Outer valve spring	11. O-ring	19. Rocker arm
4. Inner valve spring	12. Exhaust valve	20. Rocker arm shaft
5. Inner seal	13. Valve spring seat	21. Knock pin
6. Valve stem seal cap	14. Intake valve guide	22. Camshaft
7. Valve stem seal	15. Valve guide clip	23. Camchain
8. Stem seal rubber cushion	16. Intake valve	24. Dowel pin

come smooth and even, with an unblemished finish, the job is completed. Clean the valves and head with a solvent to remove the lapping compound grit after all valves have been lapped. Check for warpage of the head mating surface with a straightedge and feeler gauge. Cap or mill the head if clearance between the head and straightedge exceeds 0.002 in. (0.05 mm).

CYLINDER BORE AND PISTONS

Measure the cylinder bore diameter at the top, center, and bottom in both the fore-and-aft and side-to-side directions. Reboring will be necessary if any of the measurements exceeds 1.736 in. (125) or 2.051 in. (175), or if the cylinder bore is ta-

pered or out of round more than 0.002 in. (0.05 mm). See the specifications at the end of the chapter for piston oversizes. The bores should be honed if they have

Using a dial indicator (1) to measure cylinder bore wear (2).

been rebored or if new rings are to be used.

Measure the diameter of the piston skirt, perpendicular to the wrist pin. Pistons should be replaced when calculated clearance between the piston and cylinder is greater than 0.004 in. (0.1 mm).

If the original pistons are to be reused, remove the rings and clean the grooves using a piece of one of the old rings. Remove the carbon deposit from the piston tops. Roll the new rings around the grooves before installing them to ensure that there is sufficient clearance. The rings should roll smoothly without binding. Install the rings on the pistons using a ring expander to avoid breaking them. Make sure that the mark on the rings (if any) is facing up.

Piston and Cylinder Barrel Installation

1. Install the pistons on the connecting rods in their original positions. Be sure to use new wrist pin circlips.

2. Stagger the rings so that the gaps are 120° apart and not in line with or perpendicular to the piston boss axis.

3. Install the cylinder base gasket and two dowel pins.

Cylinder dowel pins (1).

4. Install piston bases or blocks of wood cut to suitable size under the pistons to hold them in position.

5. Compress the rings (after oiling them liberally) and carefully install the cylinder barrel over them. Take care not to damage the rings.

6. Before seating the cylinder fully, raise the cam chain through the center and hold the ends from dropping back down. Install the cylinder retaining bolt(s).

Cylinder Head Installation

1. Install the head gasket, dowel pins, and O-rings on the cylinder.

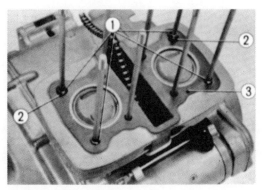

Install the dowel pins (1), O-rings (2), and head gasket (3).

2. Loosen the adjuster locknut and bolt, push the cam chain tensioner as far as it will go into the head, and lock it there with the adjuster bolt.

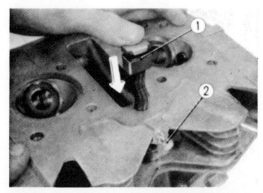

Loosen the adjuster bolt (2) and push the cam chain tensioner (1) into the head.

3. Assemble the valves, rocker arms, and camshaft into the head in reverse order of disassembly.

4. Fit the head carefully onto the cylinder.

5. To properly set the valve timing, first turn the crankshaft until the "T" mark on the alternator rotor is aligned with the timing index mark on the alternator stator. Then rotate the camshaft until the "O" mark on the face of the sprocket is at the top, and install the cam chain. The master link clip must be installed with the closed end facing the direction chain rotation.

6. Install the cylinder head nuts and tighten them gradually, in the sequence shown, to 12–15 ft lb.

Connect the cam chain when the "O" mark (1) on the cam sprocket is at the top, with the "T" mark on the alternator rotor and the timing index mark aligned.

7. Reinstall the engine and perform a complete tune-up, paying special attention to valve and cam chain adjustments. Refer to chapter 3. The valves and cam chain should be checked again after approximately 500 miles have been covered. Don't forget to refill the engine with oil.

SPLITTING THE CRANKCASES

1. Remove the engine from the frame and remove the cylinder head, barrel, and pistons as described in the preceding section on top end overhaul.
NOTE: *If desired, the cases can be split without disassembling the top end.*
2. Take out the screws and remove the left-side crankcase cover.

Left crankcase cover (1).

3. Unscrew the alternator rotor retaining bolt and remove the rotor using Honda tool no. 07011-21601 or a suitably sized bolt.
4. Take out the three screws and remove the starter clutch. Remove the master link and take off the starter chain. Re-

Using a threaded puller (1) to remove the rotor (2).

Starter chain (1).

move the set plate and pull the starter sprocket off of the crankshaft.
5. Remove the kickstart lever, take out the ten retaining screws, and remove the right-side crankcase cover.
6. Unscrew the four clutch pressure plate retaining bolts and withdraw the clutch discs and plates.

Pressure plate retaining bolts (1) and clutch assembly (2).

7. Remove the oil filter rotor locknut and then the filter retaining nut, and pull the rotor off of the crankshaft.
8. Take out the 20 mm circlip and remove the clutch center.

Oil filter rotor (1) and oil pump assembly (2).

9. Unscrew the oil pump mounting nuts and remove the oil pump assembly and clutch outer housing as an assembly. CAUTION: *Take care not to damage the crankshaft when removing the clutch housing.*

Circlip (1) and clutch center (3).

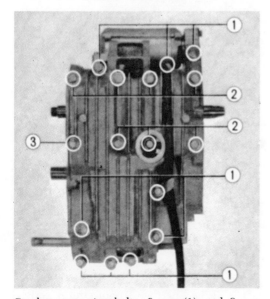

Crankcase securing bolts—6 mm (1), and 8 mm (2), 175.

10. Remove the gearshift spindle and kickstart return spring.

11. Remove the crankcase securing bolts and nuts and separate the crankcase halves with a rubber hammer. Do not neglect to remove the bolt under the oil drainplug.

Top crankcase mounting bolts (1 and 2), 125.

Bottom crankcase securing bolts—6 mm (1), and 8 mm (2), 125.

Assembling the Crankcases

Assembly is a reversal of the disassembly procedures. Observe the following points:

1. Clean the crankcase mating surfaces carefully and inspect them for scratches, signs of leaks, and other damage. Use a sealing compound on the surfaces to prevent oil leaks.

2. Don't forget to reinstall the two

dowel pins in the upper crankcase if they were removed.

CRANKSHAFT AND CONNECTING RODS

Disassembly

The crankshaft is a built-up unit with one-piece connecting rods and main bearings. It cannot be disassembled and repaired by normal means. Check for excessive wear as described below, and if any of the measurements are beyond the serviceable limits the crankshaft assembly should be replaced.

Inspection

Support the outer main bearings in V-blocks, as shown, and measure crankshaft runout 1.3 in. (30 mm) in from each end of the crankshaft with a dial indicator. (Runout equals one-half the dial indicator reading.) Maximum acceptable runout is 0.0032 in. (0.08 mm).

Support the ends of the crankshaft with V-blocks (or any other means that will hold it securely) and check the radial and axial clearance of the main bearings. Maximum acceptable axial clearance is 0.004 in. (0.1 mm), and maximum radial clearance is 0.002 in. (0.05 mm).

Measure the amount of side to side movement of the connecting rod at the small end, as shown in the accompanying illustration. Maximum permissible deflection (indicative of worn rod bearings) is 0.118 in. (3.0 mm).

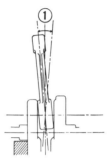

Checking the connecting rod bearings by measuring small end movement (1).

Assembly

When installing the crankshaft into the crankcase, make sure that the dowel pins in the bearing seats of the upper crankcase

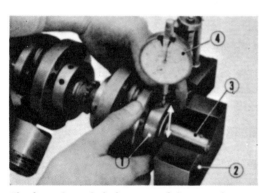

Checking the radial clearance of the main bearing (1) with a dial indicator (4).

Dowel pins (1), upper crankcase (2).

Checking axial clearance of the main bearing (1) with a dial indicator (2).

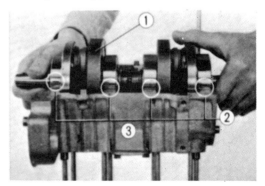

Crankshaft (1), bearing scribe lines (2), and upper crankcase (3).

are installed, and that the dowels fit into the locating holes in the main bearings. This can be made simpler by aligning the lines scribed into the outside of the bearing races with the crankcase mating surface.

CLUTCH SERVICE

Disassembly

1. Remove the kickstart lever, take out the ten retaining screws, and remove the right-side crankcase cover. Refer to the preceding section on splitting the crankcases.

2. Unscrew the four clutch pressure plate bolts and withdraw the clutch discs and plates.

3. If you wish to remove the clutch housing and hub assembly, first remove the oil filter retaining nut, and pull the filter rotor off the crankshaft.

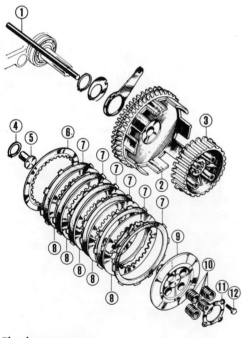

Clutch components.

1. Clutch rod
2. Clutch outer complete
3. Clutch center
4. 20 mm set ring
5. Clutch lifter joint piece
6. Clutch plate B
7. Clutch friction disc
8. Clutch plate
9. Clutch pressure plate
10. Clutch spring
11. Clutch spring retaining plate
12. 6 x 20 hex bolt

4. Take out the 20 mm circlip and remove the clutch center.

5. Unscrew the oil pump mounting nuts and remove the oil pump assembly and clutch outer housing as an assembly.

CAUTION: *Take care not to damage the crankshaft when removing the clutch housing.*

Inspection

Measure the thickness of the clutch discs and plates with a vernier caliper or micrometer. Replace the discs if they measure less than 0.0984 in. (2.5 mm), and the plates if they measure less than 0.114 in. (2.9 mm). Warpage of the plates and discs should be checked by placing them on a flat surface such as a surface plate or a plate of glass, and measuring any gaps with a feeler gauge. Maximum allowable warpage for the discs and plates is 0.02 in. (0.5 mm). Measure the free length of the clutch springs and replace them if less than 1.20 in. (30.3 mm).

Examine the primary drive gears at this time for chipping, pitting, and excessive wear; replace if necessary. Before reinstalling the plates and discs, make sure that the tabs and slots in the clutch center are in good condition.

Assembly

Assembly is a reversal of the disassembly procedures. Install the discs and plates alternately, beginning with a disc. Take care to torque the pressure plate bolts evenly. Perform a complete clutch adjustment after assembly. Refer to chapter 2.

TRANSMISSION SERVICE

Disassembly

1. Remove the engine from the frame and follow disassembly steps 2–11 under "Splitting the Crankcases."

2. Lift out the transmission mainshaft and countershaft assemblies.

3. Disassemble the gears from the shafts, taking care to lay them out in order of assembly.

Inspection

1. Examine the dogs on the respective gears and if damaged or excessively worn, the gears should be replaced. Check to make sure that the gears are free to slide smoothly on the shafts.

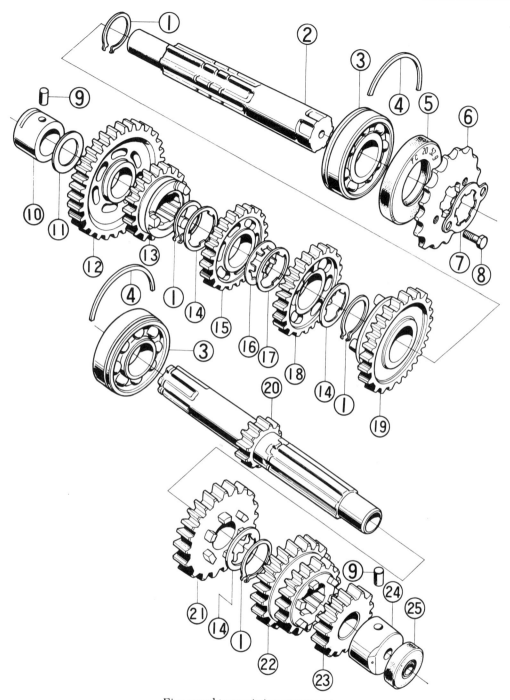

Five-speed transmission components.

1. Circlip
2. Transmission countershaft
3. Ball bearing
4. Ball bearing set ring
5. Oil seal
6. Drive sprocket
7. Drive sprocket fixing plate
8. Bolt
9. Guide pin
10. Bushing
11. Thrust washer
12. Countershaft low gear
13. Countershaft top gear
14. Thrust washer
15. Countershaft fourth gear
16. Thrust washer
17. Thrust washer
18. Countershaft third gear
19. Countershaft second gear
20. Transmission mainshaft
21. Mainshaft top gear
22. Mainshaft shifting gear
23. Mainshaft second gear
24. Bushing
25. Oil seal

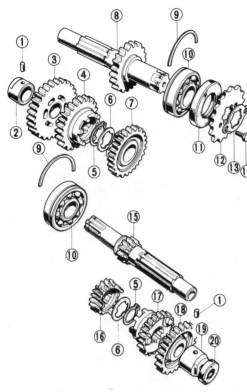

Four-speed transmission components.

1. Knock pin
2. Bushing
3. Countershaft low gear
4. Countershaft second gear
5. Circlip
6. Thrust washer
7. Countershaft third gear
8. Transmission countershaft
9. Bearing set ring
10. Ball bearing
11. Oil seal
12. Drive sprocket
13. Drive sprocket plate
14. Bolt
15. Transmission mainshaft
16. Mainshaft second gear
17. Mainshaft third gear
18. Mainshaft top gear
19. Bushing
20. Oil seal

2. Check the backlash of the mating gears, with the shaft assemblies in the case, using a dial indicator. Replace gears that are outside the limits given in the table.

	Standard Value	Serviceable Limit
1st, 2nd, 3rd gears	0.0017 ~ 0.0052 in. (0.044 ~ 0.133 mm)	Replace if over 0.008 in. (0.2 mm)
4th and 5th gears	0.0016 ~ 0.005 in. (0.042 ~ 0.126 mm)	Replace if over 0.008 in. (0.2 mm)

Measuring gear backlash with a dial indicator (1).

3. Check the gear teeth for pitting, wear, and damage. Gears must be replaced in sets.

4. Compute the gear-to-shaft clearance of the gears in the accompanying table by measuring first the shaft diameter and then the gear bore diameter, and subtracting the former from the latter. (M4 means mainshaft fourth gear, etc.)

5-SPEED TRANSMISSIONS

	Standard Value	Serviceable Limit
M4	0.0008 ~ 0.0024 in. (0.02 ~ 0.062 mm)	Replace if over 0.004 in. (0.1 mm)
M5, C1	0.0006 ~ 0.0018 in. (0.016 ~ 0.045 mm)	
C2, C3	0.0016 ~ 0.003 in. (0.04 ~ 0.082 mm)	Replace if over 0.0047 in. (0.12 mm)

4-SPEED TRANSMISSIONS

	Standard Value	Serviceable Limit
M2, C3	0.001 ~ 0.002 in. (0.029 ~ 0.053 mm)	Replace if over 0.0047 in. (0.1 mm)
C1, M4	0.0006 ~ 0.0018 in. (0.016 ~ 0.045 mm)	Replace if over 0.0047 in. (0.1 mm)

Assembly

Assemble the transmission components in reverse order of disassembly, using the accompanying illustration as a guide. It is very important that the old circlips are not reused on the transmission shafts. Check that the transmission bearing set rings are in place before installing the shaft assemblies. Assemble the crankcases as previously described.

SHIFTER MECHANISM

Disassembly

1. Follow disassembly steps 1 and 2 under the preceding section on transmission service.

2. Remove the neutral indicator switch limit arm and then remove the switch from the top of the crankcase.

3. Pull out the shift drum guide pin clips and guide pins.

4. Unscrew the 6 mm bolt and remove

Shift drum limit arm (1) and neutral limit arm (2).

The right shift fork (1), center shift fork (2), left shift fork (3), and the guide pin clips (4).

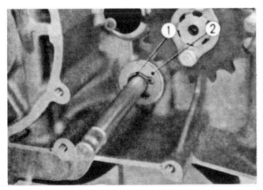

Shift drum spindle circlip (1) and washer (2).

the shift drum limit arm and limit arm plate. Withdraw the shift drum.

5. The shift spindle and return spring can be removed after the circlip has been removed from the end of the spindle.

Inspection

1. Check that the shift spindle and arm are not bent or twisted.

2. Examine the shift fork fingers for damage and excessive wear. The forks must be in good condition for the transmission to shift properly. Replace the forks if the fingers measure less than 0.200 in., or if the fork bore inside diameter is greater than 1.342 in.

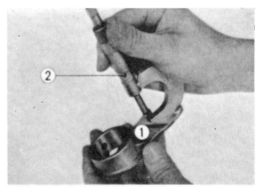

Measuring the thickness of the shift fork fingers (1) with a micrometer (2).

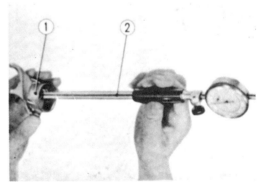

Measuring the shift fork bore diameter (1) with a dial indicator (2).

3. Check that the shift drum tracks and shift fork guide pins are not excessively worn.

4. Check the springs for breakage and adequate tension.

Assembly

1. Install the shift drum from the right side of the upper crankcase and assemble the shift forks onto the drum as shown.

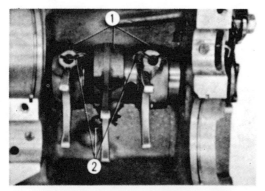

Install the shift forks (1) and pin clips (2) in this position (5-speed models).

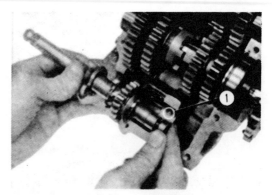

Removing the kick-start assembly, showing the locating pin (1).

Install the shift forks (2) and pin clips (1) in this position (4-speed models).

2. Install the shift fork guide pins and pin clips.

3. Assemble the neutral switch into the shift drum.

4. Install the shift drum limit arm and plate.

5. Install the shift return spring in the lower crankcase.

6. Install the shift spindle and return spring from the right side of the lower crankcase. The shift spindle side stopper and oil seal should be installed from the left end of the spindle. Then install the set ring.

7. Install the transmission shaft assemblies, making sure that the bearing set rings are in place, and assemble the crankcases as previously described.

KICKSTART MECHANISM SERVICE

The kickstart shaft and ratchet assembly can be removed after the shifter mechanism components have been disassembled from the crankcase. A slipping ratchet assembly (normally the only cause for kickstart failure) must be replaced.

350

ENGINE REMOVAL AND INSTALLATION

1. Drain the engine oil.

2. Turn the fuel tap off, disconnect the fuel lines, and remove the gas tank.

3. Remove the entire exhaust system, as a unit, from each side.

4. Remove the footpeg and shift lever, and take off the left-side rear crankcase cover.

5. Separate the drive chain at the master link and disconnect the clutch cable from the release lever.

6. Back the rear brake adjuster nut off so that the brake pedal drops down and out of the way.

7. Disconnect the throttle cables from the throttle sides at the carburetors.

NOTE: *On the SL 350K1 and K2, unscrew the carburetor tops and lift out the slides. Tie them out of the way.*

8. Disconnect the electrical leads at the connectors. Refer to the accompanying illustration.

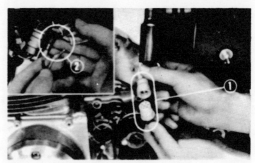

The electrical lead connector (1) and contact breaker connectors.

9. Disconnect the wires from the spark plugs and tuck them up out of the way.

10. Disconnect the starter motor cable from the starter solenoid (if applicable).

11. Disconnect the tachometer cable from the tachometer drive at the engine.

12. Unscrew the engine mounting bolts and remove the engine from the right side.

Engine mounting bolts.

Installation is a reversal of the removal procedure. The following points should be noted:

1. Do not neglect to reconnect the battery ground cable when installing the engine mounting bolts.

2. The chain master link clip should be installed so that the closed end faces the direction of forward rotation.

3. Make sure that the steel ball has been installed in the clutch release lever before reinstalling the crankcase cover. And replace engine oil.

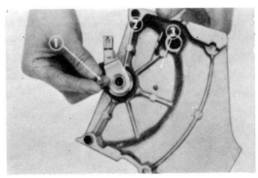

Steel ball (1), clutch release lever (2), and crankcase cover (3).

TOP END OVERHAUL

Cylinder Head Removal

1. Unscrew the eight cap nuts and lift off the cam cover.

2. Remove the alternator cover and ignition points cover.

3. Take out the screws and remove the points breaker plate assembly. Unscrew the bolt from the center of the breaker cam and remove the ignition advance unit.

Points breaker plate assembly (1) and the ignition advance unit (2).

4. Remove the rocker arm shaft end nuts (valve adjuster locknuts) and then take out the screws and remove the cylinder head side covers. Remove the rocker arm shafts.

Rocker arm shaft end nuts (1), rocker arm shafts (2), cylinder head side cover (3), and rocker arms (4).

5. Unbolt and remove the cam chain tensioner assembly from the rear of the cylinder barrel.

6. Rotate the crankshaft until one of the cam chain sprocket retaining bolts is accessible, and unscrew the bolt. Then rotate the crankshaft one full turn and remove the remaining bolt.

NOTE: *Special bolts are used for this application and are marked on their heads with the number "9". Do not use any substitute bolts.*

7. Withdraw the camshaft through the

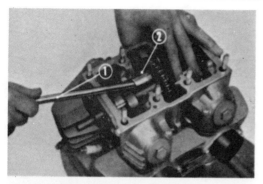

Unscrewing the cam sprocket bolt (2).

Cam case mounting screws (1) and the cam case (2).

cam chain sprocket, from the right side of the engine.

8. Take out the four screws and remove the cam case.

9. Remove the spark plugs and unscrew the two head bolts.

10. Lift the cylinder head off of the cylinder.

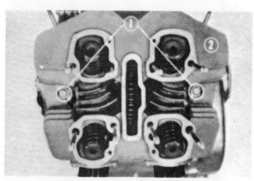

Cylinder head bolts (1) and the cylinder head (2).

Cylinder Barrel and Piston Removal

1. Carefully lift the cylinder off of the crankcase. Take care to prevent the pistons from being damaged on the studs as the cylinder is withdrawn over them.

2. Remove the wrist pin circlips from the pistons.

CAUTION: *Do not allow the circlips to fall into the crankcase. To avoid having to split the cases to retrieve a clip, cover the crankcase opening with a cloth.*

3. Push the wrist pins out of the pistons. Mark the pistons, inside the skirt, so that they can be reinstalled in their original positions.

Component Inspection and Service

CAMSHAFT

Carefully examine the cam lobes for excessive wear and scoring. Temporarily reinstall the camshaft back into the cylinder head and measure the side clearance with a dial indicator. If side clearance exceeds 0.04 in. (0.2 mm), obtain a special 0.2 mm shim available from Honda dealers for use with the camshaft, and install it during reassembly.

Using a dial indicator (1) to measure side-clearance of the camshaft (2).

Using a micrometer (1) to measure cam height (2).

Measure the height of the cam lobes and replace the camshaft if the dimension of either the intake or exhaust lobes is less than 1.444 in. (36.68 mm). The diameter of the left and right bearing surfaces of the camshaft should not measure less than 0.863 in. (20.050 mm). The inside diameter of the left and right cylinder head covers, measured in both the "X" and "Y" directions as shown, should not exceed 0.868 in. (21.920 mm). Replace if necessary. Minor defects on the cams can be finished off with a fine oilstone.

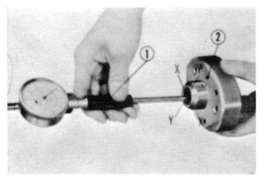

Using a dial indicator (1) to measure the inside diameter of the cylinder head side-cover (2).

VALVE ROCKER ASSEMBLY

Measure the diameter of the rocker arm shafts. Replace the shafts if less than 0.508 in (12.9 mm). Check the fit of the rocker arms on their shafts, and make sure that the rocker arm pads (cam contact surface) are not excessively worn.

CYLINDER HEAD AND VALVES

Compress the springs (Honda spring compressor no. 07031-25001) and remove the collars, retainers, springs, and valves. To check valve stem and guide wear, insert the valve into the guide and measure clearance in both the "X" and "Y" directions, as shown, with a dial indicator. If clearance is greater than 0.003 in. (0.08

Checking valve guide clearance with a dial indicator (2).

mm) (intake valves), or 0.004 in. (0.09 mm) (exhaust valves), the valve and guide should be replaced as a set. The replacement guide should be one that is oversize, for a proper fit. Guides can be driven out and installed using Honda service tool no. 07046-25901 or a suitably sized drift. Take care to install the guide straight. The guides should be reamed with tool no. 07008-28601 after installation. Use the reamer carefully, with sufficient lubrication, and recheck valve clearance when completed.

Using a drift (1) to drive a valve guide out of the head (2).

Valve guide reamer (1).

The valve stem diameter should be measured at the top, center, and bottom using a micrometer. Minimum intake valve stem diameter is 0.274 in. (6.955 mm), and minimum exhaust diameter is 0.273 in. (6.935 mm). Maximum valve contact face width is 0.08 in. (2.0 mm). Do not attempt to reface the valves or refinish the valve stem ends, as these surfaces have a thin stellite facing that will be destroyed if cut. If the valve seat is burnt, worn, or damaged in any way it should be recut. Valve seat angle 45°. Seat width should be within 0.04–0.05 in. (1–1.3 mm).

Carefully scrape carbon deposits from the combustion chambers and thoroughly clean the cylinder head. Before the valves are installed, whether they are the original ones or new, they should be lapped into their seats so that a perfect seal will be obtained. To properly lap a valve, first place three small dabs of lapping compound around the valve face. Insert the valve into the guide, and, using a lapping tool (available at most auto supply stores), rotate the valve back and forth between the palms of your hands. Reposition the valve every few seconds, and examine the valve face and seat surfaces. When they have become smooth and even, with an unblemished finish, the job is completed. Clean the valves and head with a solvent to remove the lapping compound grit after all the valves have been lapped.

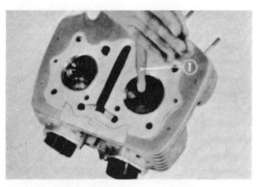

Valve lapping tool (1).

It is a good idea at this time to replace the valve springs. However, if the height of the original springs is not less than 1.547 in. (39.3 mm) (inner springs) or 1.882 in. (47.8 mm) (outer springs), they can be reused if desired.

NOTE: *Be sure to install the springs with the smaller pitch coils toward the head.*

Place a straightedge on the cylinder head surface and measure the clearance with a feeler gauge at several points to determine head warpage or distortion. If the clearance at any point exceeds 0.002 in. (0.05 mm), the head surface should be milled or lapped flat. Lapping can be accomplished using a large, flat oilstone on the head surface with a figure eight motion. It may be helpful to first coat the surface with machinist's blue so that you can observe the removal of high spots.

Make sure that the head is clean and

The valve springs (1) should be installed with the smaller pitch (2) toward the head.

Using a feeler gauge (1) and straightedge (2) to measure cylinder head warpage.

free from grit and install the valves as removed. Lubricate the valve stems before inserting them into the guides.

Cylinder Bore and Pistons

Measure the cylinder bore diameter at the top, center, and bottom of the cylinders in both the fore-and-aft and side-to-side directions. If any measurement exceeds 2.524 in. (64.1 mm), or if bore taper or ovality is greater than 0.002 in. (0.05 mm), the cylinders should be rebored. See the specifications at the end of the chapter for piston oversizes. The cylinders should be honed after boring or whenever new rings are to be used.

Measure the diameter of the piston skirt, perpendicular to the wrist pin. Pistons should be replaced when less than 2.515 in. (63.9 mm), or if they are scored or damaged in any way. The piston wrist pin hole should be measured at both ends and 90° apart, and the diameter should be no greater than 0.594 in. (15.08 mm). The wrist pin should be a hand press-fit in the piston and connecting rod.

If the original pistons are to be reused,

remove the rings and clean the grooves using a piece of one of the old rings. Remove the carbon deposit from the tops of the pistons. Roll the new rings around the grooves before installing them to ensure that there is sufficient clearance. The rings should roll smoothly without binding. Install the rings on the pistons using a ring expander, if possible, to avoid breaking them. Make sure that the mark on the rings is facing up when installed.

Piston and Cylinder Barrel Installation

1. Install the pistons on the connecting rods in their original positions. Be sure to use new wrist pin circlips.
2. Stagger the rings so that the gaps are 120° apart and not in line with or perpendicular to the piston boss axis.
3. Install the cylinder base gasket and two dowel pins, and check to make sure that the O-ring and cam chain guide are installed on the cylinder skirt.
4. Fit piston bases, or blocks of wood cut to suitable size, under the pistons to hold them in position. Compress the rings (after oiling them liberally) and carefully install the cylinder barrel over them. Take care not to damage the rings.
5. Before seating the cylinder fully, raise the cam chain through the center and stick a screwdriver through the chain to keep it from dropping back down.

Cylinder Head Installation

1. Install the head gasket onto the cylinder.
2. Check to make sure that the two dowel pins are in position.
3. Mount the cylinder head on the cylinder while pulling the cam chain through the center of the head.
4. To properly set the valve timing, first align the "LT" mark on the alternator rotor with the timing index mark on the stator. The left piston will then be at TDC. Fit the cam sprocket into the chain so that the cutout (flat spot with the "L" mark) is at the top, and fit the camshaft through the sprocket and into position. Bolt the sprocket onto the camshaft.
NOTE: *The two sprocket retaining bolts are different, and their positions must not be reversed. Refer to the accompanying illustration.*

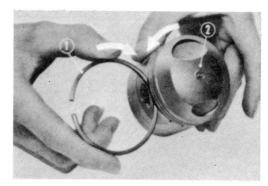
Roll the rings (1) around the piston grooves to check for sufficient clearance.

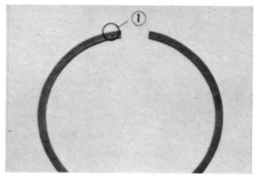
The mark on the rings (1) should face up when installed.

The "L" mark (1) on the cam sprocket (2) should be at the top.

The cam sprocket mounting bolts (1 and 3) and the cam sprocket (2).

Camshaft (1), cam sprocket (2), and pin (3).

5. Install the rocker arms and rocker arm shafts.

6. Install the side-covers.

7. Install the ignition advance unit (taking care to locate it correctly on the camshaft with the dowel pin) and the breaker plate assembly.

8. Install and tighten the two 6 mm nuts near the spark plug holes.

9. Install the cam cover with the head nuts and tighten the nuts evenly, in the sequence shown, to 13–14.5 ft lbs.

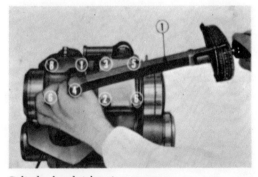

Cylinder head tightening sequence.

10. Install the cam chain tensioner on the cylinder.

11. Reinstall the engine in the frame and perform a complete tune-up, paying special attention to the valve and cam chain adjustments. Refer to chapter three. The valves and cam chain should be checked again after approximately 500 miles have been covered. Don't forget to refill the engine with oil.

SPLITTING THE CRANKCASES

1. Remove the engine from the frame and remove the cylinder head, barrel, and pistons as described in the previous section.

NOTE: *If desired, the cases can be split without disassembling the top end.*

2. Lift the cam chain roller pin and rubber mounts out of the top of the case (between the connecting rods). (When reinstalling, the cutout on the roller pin must be positioned toward the top.)

3. Remove the kick-start lever, take out the mounting screws, and remove the right-side crankcase cover.

4. Take out the circlip and remove the oil filter cap. The cap can be pulled out easily after a 6 mm (10 mm head) bolt is screwed into it.

5. Bend back the locktab and unscrew the 16 mm oil filter rotor retaining nut. Remove the rotor.

6. Unscrew the four clutch pressure plate bolts and remove the clutch springs, plates, and discs.

7. Take out the 25 mm circlip and remove the clutch center hub.

8. Bend back the locktab and unscrew the oil pump mounting bolts.

9. Withdraw the clutch housing and oil pump as a unit, taking care not to damage the end of the crankshaft as the housing is pulled off. (It may be necessary to remove the oil filter cap and rotor for additional clearance.)

10. Remove the gearshift spindle.

11. Disconnect the lead from the neutral indicator switch.

12. Take out the screws and remove the left crankcase cover.

13. Unscrew the retaining bolt and pull off the alternator rotor using Honda service tool no. 07011-21601 or a suitably sized bolt.

14. Remove the starter clutch sprocket set plate and take off the clutch sprocket and starter motor sprocket as a unit (except SL).

15. Unscrew the two crankcase securing bolts on the upper side and the twelve bolts on the lower crankcase. Lift the lower crankcase half away. If necessary, tap the crankcases with a rubber mallet to break the joint seal.

Assembling the Crankcases

Assembly is a reversal of the disassembly procedures. Observe the following points:

1. Clean the crankcase mating surfaces carefully and inspect them for scratches, signs of leaks, and other damage. Use a

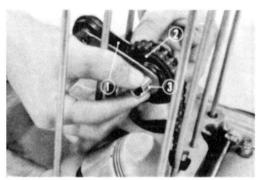

Cam chain roller bracket (1), chain roller (2), and roller pin (3).

Clutch housing (1) and oil pump (2).

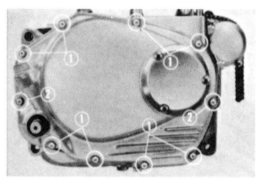

Right-side crankcase cover mounting screws (1 and 2).

Neutral switch connection (1) and neutral switch (2).

Circlip (1), oil filter cap (2), circlip pliers (3), and a 6 mm bolt (4, used to pull off the cap).

Left crankcase cover (1).

Clutch assembly (1).

Alternator rotor (1) and rotor puller (2).

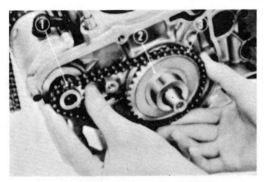

Starter motor sprocket (1), starter clutch sprocket (2), and starter chain (3).

Upper crankcase securing bolts (1).

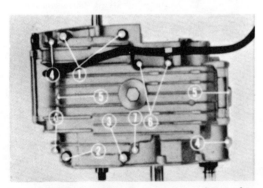

Lower crankcase tightening sequence. (Note that the different numbered bolts have different lengths.)

sealing compound on the surfaces to prevent oil leaks.

2. Make sure that the kick-starter is properly engaged in the lower crankcase.

3. Handle the starter and alternator cables with care so that the clamps won't be damaged.

4. Tighten the alternator rotor bolt to 16–17.5 ft lbs.

CRANKSHAFT AND CONNECTING RODS

Disassembly

The crankshaft is a built-up unit with one-piece connecting rods and main bearings. It cannot be disassembled and repaired by normal means. Check for excessive wear as described below. If any of the measurements are beyond the serviceable limits the crankshaft assembly should be replaced.

The crankshaft can be lifted out of the case after the main bearing caps have been unbolted and removed.

Inspection

Support the center main bearings in a V-block and measure the amount of runout at the end of the crankshaft and the counterweight with a dial indicator. Maximum allowable runout is 0.006 in. (0.15 mm), at the shaft end, and 0.012 in. (0.3 mm) at the counterweight.

NOTE: *Runout equals one-half the dial indicator reading.*

Support the crankshaft securely at two points and measure the radial (up-and-down) clearance of the main and connecting rod bearings with a dial indicator. Bearing clearance must not exceed 0.002 in. (0.05 mm).

Checking main bearing radial clearance with a dial indicator (1).

Check the side clearance of the rod bearings with a feeler gauge, as shown. Side clearance should not exceed 0.023 in. (0.60 mm).

Measure the inside diameter of the connecting rod wrist pin bores with an inside micrometer or dial indicator. A measure of over 0.593 in. (15.07 mm) indicates excessive wear.

Checking the connecting rod bearing side clearance with a feeler gauge (1).

Dowel pin grooves (1) in the upper crankcase (2).

Assembly

When installing the crankshaft into the crankcase, make sure that the dowel pin in each crankcase bearing seat is firmly installed, and that the pins fit into the locating holes in the main bearings. Tighten the four center bearing cap bolts gradually and evenly, in a diagonal sequence, to 16–17.5 ft lbs.

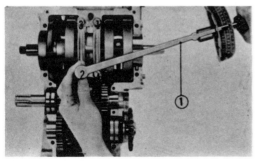

Main bearing cap tightening sequence. Use a torque wrench (1) to tighten the bolts to 16–17.5 ft lbs.

CLUTCH SERVICE

Disassembly

1. Remove the kick-start lever, take out the ten retaining screws, and remove the right-side crankcase cover. Refer to the section on splitting the crankcases.

2. Unscrew the four clutch pressure plate bolts and withdraw the clutch discs and plates.

3. If you wish to remove the clutch housing and hub assembly, first take out the 25 mm circlip and withdraw the clutch hub (center). Next, bend back the locktab and unscrew the oil pump mounting bolts. Remove the oil pump and clutch housing as an assembly.

CAUTION: *Take care not to damage the crankshaft when removing the clutch housing. It may be necessary to remove the oil filter cap and rotor to provide additional clearance.*

Inspection

Measure the thickness of the clutch discs with a vernier caliper or micrometer. Replace the discs if they measure less than 0.091 in. (2.3 mm). Warpage of the plates can be checked by placing them on a flat surface such as a surface plate or a plate of glass, and measuring any gaps with a feeler gauge. Maximum allowable warpage is 0.012 in. (0.3 mm). Measure the free-length of the clutch springs and replace them if less than 1.200 in. (30.50 mm).

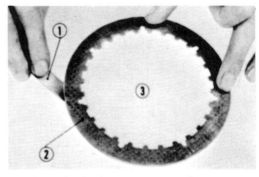

Checking clutch plate warpage. Feeler gauge (1), clutch plate (2), surface plate (3).

Examine the primary drive gears at this time for chipping, pitting, and excessive wear, and replace if necessary. Before reinstalling the plates and discs, make sure that the tabs and slots in the clutch center are in good condition.

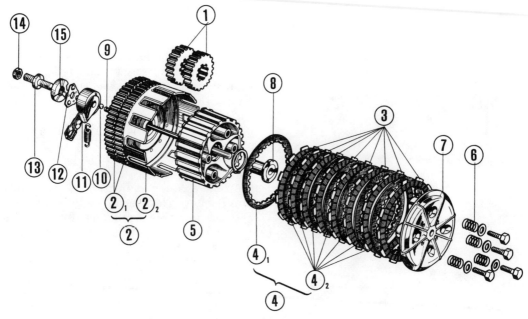

Exploded view of the clutch assembly.

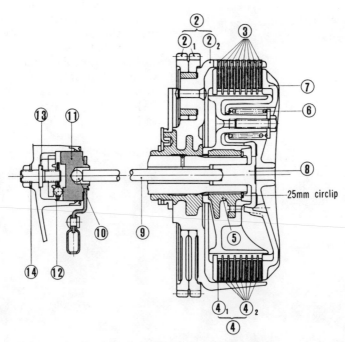

25mm circlip

Sectional view of the clutch assembly.

1. Primary drive gear
2. Clutch housing complete
2_1. Primary driven gear
2_2. Clutch housing
3. Clutch friction disc (8 ea.)
4. Clutch plate
4_1. Clutch plate A

4_2. Clutch plate B
5. Clutch center
6. Clutch spring
7. Clutch pressure plate
8. Clutch lifter joint piece
9. Clutch lifter rod
10. No. 10 steel ball

11. Clutch lever
12. Steel ball (clutch ball retainer)
13. Clutch adjuster
14. Clutch adjuster locknut
15. Clutch adjusting cam

Assembly

Assembly is a reversal of the disassembly procedure. Install the discs and plates alternately, beginning with a disc. Take care to torque the pressure plate bolts evenly. Perform a complete clutch adjustment after assembly. Refer to chapter two.

TRANSMISSION SERVICE

Disassembly

1. Remove the engine from the frame and follow disassembly steps 3–15 under "Splitting the Crankcases."
2. Lift out the transmission mainshaft and countershaft assemblies.
3. Disassemble the mainshaft in the following order: remove the needle roller bearing, the M5 and M2-M3 gears, the circlip, the thrust washer, and the M4 gear.
4. Disassemble the countershaft in the following order: remove the needle roller bearings, the circlip thrust washer that retains the C3 gear, the C3 and C2 gears, and the C5 circlip and gear.

NOTE: *On later engines (from CB/CL 350E-1042395 and all SL engines) a 25 mm thrust washer and a lockwasher are installed between the C2 and C3 gears. Remove the C3 gear first and then take off the washers.*

Inspection

1. Examine the dogs on the respective gears and, if damaged or excessively worn, the gears should be replaced. Check to make sure that the gears are free to slide smoothly on the shafts.
2. Check the gear teeth for pitting, wear, and damage. Gears must be replaced in sets.
3. Compute the gear-to-shaft clearance of the gears in the accompanying table by measuring first the shaft diameter and then the gear bore diameter, and subtracting the former from the latter. (M4 means mainshaft fourth gear, etc.)

	(in./mm)	
	Standard Value	Serviceable Limit
M4, M5	0.0008–0.0024 in./ 0.02–0.062 mm	Replace if over 0.004 in./0.10 mm
C1	0.0008–0.0020 in./ 0.02–0.054 mm	Replace if over 0.004 in./0.10 mm
C2, C3	0.0016–0.002 in./ 0.04–0.054 mm	Replace if over 0.004 in./0.10 mm

Assembly

Assemble the transmission components in reverse order of disassembly, using the accompanying illustration as a guide. Observe the following points:

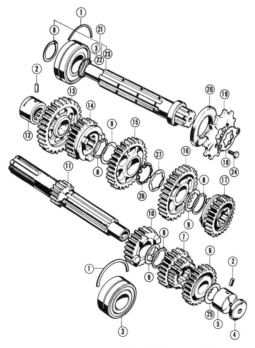

1. Bearing setting ring
2. Bearing dowel pin
3. Ball bearing
4. Oil seal
5. Needle bearing
6. Mainshaft top gear
7. Mainshaft second & third gear
8. 25 mm, circlip
9. 25 mm, thrust washer
10. Mainshaft fourth gear
11. Transmission mainshaft
12. Needle bearing
13. Countershaft low gear
14. Countershaft fourth gear
15. Countershaft third gear
16. Countershaft second gear
17. Countershaft top gear
18. Drive sprocket fixing plate
19. Drive sprocket
20. Oil seal
21. Transmission countershaft
22. O-ring
23. Transmission countershaft
24. Bolt
25. 20 mm, thrust washer
26. Lockwasher
27. 25 mm, thrust washer B

Exploded view of the transmission.

1. Use only new circlips, and make sure that they are properly seated in their grooves.

2. Make sure that the thrust washers and circlips are installed on the M4, C2, and C3 gears.

3. When installing the bearings on the shafts, be sure to install the bearing with the oil groove on the countershaft, and the bearing without the groove on the mainshaft.

4. Check to make sure that the bearing set rings and dowel pins are in place before installing the shaft assemblies in the crankcase.

5. After the mainshaft and countershaft assemblies are in place, check the backlash of the mating gears with a dial indicator. Maximum allowable backlash is 0.008 in. (0.2 mm) for all gears.

Checking gear backlash with a dial indicator.

6. Check to make sure that the left shift fork is fitted to the C4 gear, the right shift fork to the C5 gear, and the center fork to the M2-M3 gear.

7. Assemble the crankcases as previously described.

SHIFTER MECHANISM

Disassembly

1. Follow disassembly steps one and two under the preceding section on transmission service.

2. Remove the neutral indicator switch rotor and the shift drum limit arm.

3. Pull out the shift drum guide pin clips and guide pins.

4. Withdraw the shift drum from the case by gently tapping the case on the neutral switch side.

Inspection

1. Examine the shift fork fingers for damage and excessive wear. Measure the thickness of the fingers and replace the fork if less than 0.181 in. (4.6 mm) (right and left forks), or 0.220 in. (5.6 mm) (center fork).

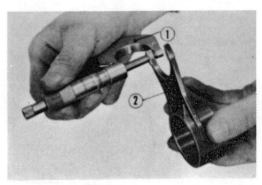

Measuring the shift fork fingers with a micrometer (1).

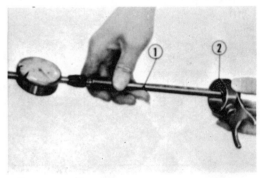

Measuring the shift fork bore with a dial indicator (1).

2. Measure the diameter of the shift fork bore. Maximum allowable diameter is 1.577 in. (40.075 mm).

3. Measure the diameter of the shift drum and replace it if over 1.571 in. (39.9 mm).

4. Check to see that the shift drum tracks and shift fork guide pins are not excessively worn.

Assembly

1. Install the shift drum and forks into the crankcase and make sure the forks are positioned properly. Refer to the accompanying illustration.

2. Install the shift fork guide pins and clips. Make sure that the clips are securely set.

3. Reassemble the remaining parts in re-

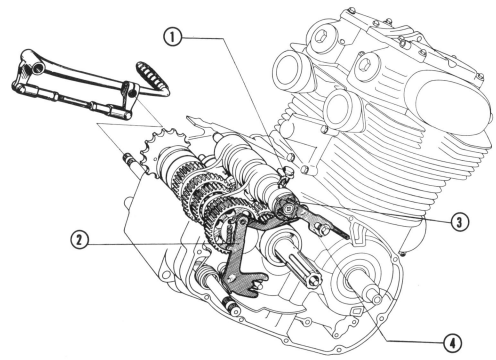

Shifter mechanism. Neutral stopper (1), shift arm (2), drum limit plate (3), and shift drum limit arm (4).

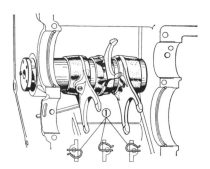

Install the shift forks and guide pin clips (1) in this position.

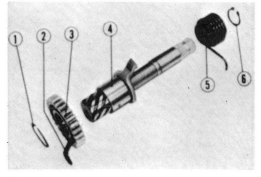

Kick-start components.

1. Circlip
2. Friction spring
3. Kick-start pinion
4. Kick-start spindle
5. Spring
6. Circlip

verse order of disassembly. Check to see that the action of the shifter mechanism is smooth.

KICK-START MECHANISM SERVICE

CB, CL, and 1970 SL Models

The kick-start shaft and pinion assembly can be removed after the crankcases have been split. If the shaft and pinion are damaged or visibly worn, they should be replaced.

SL 350K1 and K2

The primary kick-start mechanism used on these models allows the engine to be started in any gear with the clutch disengaged. To remove the kick-start shaft and gears the crankcases must be separated. Check all components for wear and damage, and replace as necessary.

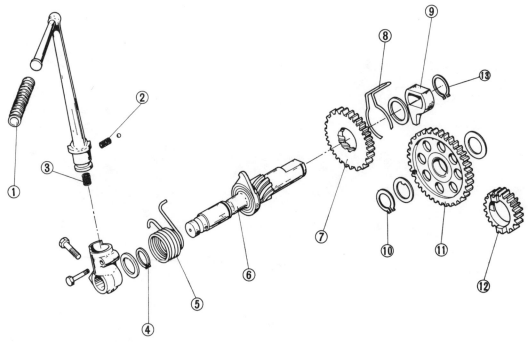

Kick-start components (SL 350).

1. Kick-starter rubber	6. Spindle	11. Idle gear
2. Stopper spring	7. Pinion	12. Kick-starter gear
3. Knuckle spring	8. Friction spring	13. Circlip
4. Circlip	9. Spindle stopper	
5. Kick-starter spring	10. Circlip	

450

ENGINE REMOVAL AND INSTALLATION

1. Drain the engine oil.

2. Turn the fuel tap off, disconnect the fuel lines, and remove the gas tank.

3. Disconnect the throttle cables from the throttle linkage at the carburetors.

4. Remove the air filter assemblies, loosen the carburetor-to-intake tube clamps, and remove the carburetors.

5. Remove the entire exhaust system, as a unit, from each side.

6. Remove the footpeg and shift lever, and take off the left-side rear crankcase cover. Separate the chain at the master link and disconnect the clutch cable from the release lever.

7. Uncouple the engine electrical leads at the connectors. Refer to the accompanying illustration.

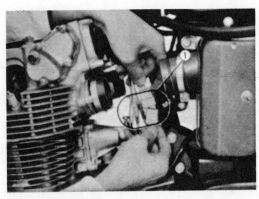

Electrical lead connectors (1).

8. Disconnect the wires from the spark plugs and tuck them up out of the way.

9. Disconnect the starter motor cable from the starter solenoid, and disconnect the tachometer cable from the cylinder head.

10. Unscrew the thirteen engine mounting bolts and remove the engine from the left side.

Engine mounting bolts (1–4).

Removing the cam chain (1) with a chain cutter (2).

Installation is a reversal of the removal procedure. Note the following points:

1. Do not forget to connect the battery ground cable when installing the engine mounting bolts.

2. The chain master link clip should be installed so that the closed end faces the direction of forward rotation.

3. Make sure that the steel ball has been installed in the clutch release lever before reinstalling the crankcase cover.

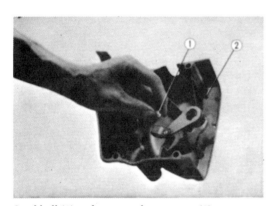

Steel ball (1) and rear crankcase cover (2).

TOP END OVERHAUL
Cylinder Head Removal

1. Remove the front and rear cam covers.

2. Rotate the crankshaft slowly and examine the cam chain links until the master link is located. It can be identified by its brighter color and crimped pin heads (rather than the normal flat heads). The master link should then be removed using Honda tool no. 07050-28303. Observe the following precautions:

    a. Disconnect the chain from the intake side.

    b. Take care not to drop the master link into the engine.

    c. Attach a length of wire to each end of the cam chain to prevent it from falling into the crankcase.

3. Gradually loosen the eight cylinder head nuts in reverse order of the tightening sequence.

Cylinder head tightening sequence. Cap nuts (1).

4. Lift the cylinder head off the cylinder barrel.

Cylinder Barrel and Piston Removal

1. Carefully lift the cylinder barrel off the crankcase. Take care to prevent the pistons from being damaged on the studs as the cylinder is withdrawn over them.

2. Remove the wrist pin circlips from the pistons.

CAUTION: *Do not allow the circlips to fall into the crankcase. To avoid having to split the cases to retrieve a clip, cover the crankcase opening with a cloth.*

3. Remove the wrist pins from the pistons. Mark the pistons, inside the skirt, so that they can be reinstalled in their original positions.

Component Inspection and Service

CAMSHAFTS

The camshafts and cam followers can be removed, if necessary, in the following manner:

Intake Side:

1. Remove the cam follower shaft (valve adjuster) locknut from the right and left sides.

2. Remove the right and left cylinder head side covers.

3. Withdraw the intake camshaft.

Exhaust Side:

1. Loosen the locknut from the right side and remove the tachometer drive.

2. Remove the ignition points cover. Take out the screws and remove the breaker plate assembly.

3. Unscrew the bolt from the center of the breaker cam and remove the ignition advance unit.

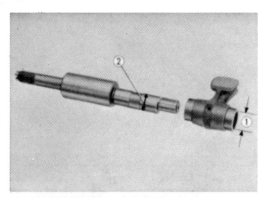

Cam follower bearing diameter (1) and cam follower shaft journal diameter (2).

4. Withdraw the exhaust camshaft.

Carefully inspect the cam lobes for scoring and wear, and check the camshaft dimensions using the accompanying chart. Inspect the cam sprockets (and dampers) for worn teeth and other damage, and replace the camshafts if necessary. Replace the cam followers if they are damaged in any way.

Measuring cam lift. Dial indicator (1), camshaft (2), and V-blocks (3).

CYLINDER HEAD AND VALVES

To remove the valves and torsion bar valve springs, first hold the torsion bar arm in the direction shown on the end of the bar to relieve the load on the retaining bolt. Then unscrew the bolt, allow the bar to return slowly to the unloaded position, and withdraw it.

CAUTION: *Do not interchange the torsion bar components from side to side or front to rear. Do not scratch or mark the bars in any way. Tag the components for identification upon disassembly.*

To remove the valves, first remove the collars and valve spring retainers. Loosen the bolts and remove the valve guide stopper and guide seal cap. Withdraw the valves.

Replace valves as necessary. When replacing valves due to worn stems, it is wise to also replace the valve guides. The replacement guides should be slightly

Item	Standard Value	Serviceable Limit
1. Cam follower bearing diameter	0.4016–0.4023 in./10.20–10.218 mm	Replace if over 0.4047 in./10.28 mm
2. Cam follower shaft journal	0.3992–0.4009 in./10.166–10.184 mm	Replace if under 0.3976 in./10.10 mm
3. Camshaft journals, intake and exhaust	0.8648–0.8654 in./21.967–21.980 mm	Replace if under 0.8622 in./21.92 mm
4. Cam lift, intake and exhaust	0.1846–0.1853 in./4.688–4.728 mm	Replace if under 0.1830 in./4.65 mm
5. Breaker point shaft run-out	0.0004 in. max/0.01 mm	Replace if over 0.002 in./0.05 mm

Torsion bar arm (1).

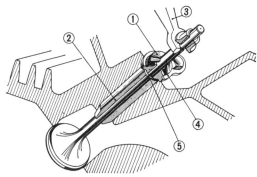

1. Valve guide seal cap   4. Valve guide stop
2. Valve guide   5. O-ring
3. Forked arm

these surfaces have a thin stellite facing that will be destroyed if cut.

The valves can be checked using the accompanying chart as a guide.

Carefully scrape carbon deposits from the combustion chambers and thoroughly clean the cylinder head. Before the valves are installed, whether they are original or new ones, they should be lapped into their seats so that a perfect seal will be obtained. To properly lap a valve, first place three small dabs of lapping compound around the valve face. Insert the valve into the guide and, using a lapping tool (available at most auto supply stores), rotate the valve back and forth lightly by rotating the handle of the lapping tool between the palms of your hands. Reposition the valve every few seconds and examine the valve face and seat surfaces. When they have become smooth and even, with an unblemished finish, the job is complete. Clean the valves and head with a solvent to remove the lapping compound grit after all valves have been lapped.

Place a straightedge on the cylinder head surface and measure the clearance with a feeler gauge at several points to determine head warpage or distortion. If the clearance at any point exceeds 0.002 in. (0.05 mm), the head surface should be milled or lapped flat. Lapping can be accomplished by using a large, flat oilstone on the head surface with a figure eight motion. It may be helpful to first coat the surface with machinist's blue so you can observe the removal of the high spots.

Make sure that the head is clean and free from grit and install the valves as removed. Lubricate the valve stems before inserting them into the guides. Install the valve springs in the following manner:

oversize and new O-rings should be used. Always ream the guides and check valve fit after installation.

If the valve seat is burned, worn, or damaged in any way, it should be recut. Valve seat angle is 45°. Seat width should be within 0.040–0.050 in. (1.0–1.3 mm). Maximum allowable seat width is 0.079 in. (2.0 mm).

NOTE: *Do not attempt to reface the valves or refinish the valve stem ends, as*

Item	Standard Value	Serviceable Limit
1. Valve stem diameter intake	0.2746–0.2751 in./6.974–6.988 mm	Replace if under 0.2740 in./6.96 mm
2. Valve stem diameter, exhaust	0.2743–0.2749 in./6.968–6.982 mm	Replace if under 0.2736 in./6.95 mm
3. Straightness of valve stem	Within 0.0008 in./0.02 mm	Replace if over 0.0008 in./0.02 mm
4. Concentricity of valve face °	0.0012 in./0.03 mm	Replace if over 0.0012 in./0.03 mm
5. Valve guide diameter and exhaust	0.2756–0.2760 in./7.0–7.01 mm	Replace if over 0.2776 in./7.05 mm

° **Run-out in this case equals the full dial indicator reading (true indicated reading).**

Measuring cylinder head warpage with a feeler gauge (1) and straightedge (2).

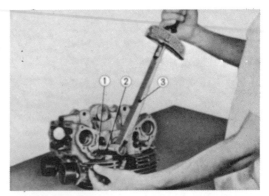

Setting the torsion bar with a torque wrench. Refer to the text. Torsion bar arm (1), torque wrench attachment (2), and torque wrench (3).

1. Assemble the torsion bars and their arms.

NOTE: *There are two types of torsion bars; they must not be interchanged. Refer to the accompanying illustration.*

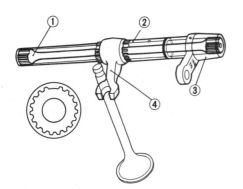

Torsion bar components.

1. Torsion bar
2. Torsion bar housing
3. Torsion bar holder arm
4. Torsion bar forked arm

2. Fit the torsion bars into the cylinder head and install the forked arms on the bars from the inside.

3. Fit the forked arm into the valve stem and check for smooth movement. If the arm is binding, the valve stem may be bent.

4. Check to make sure that the valve guide seal cap is not loose.

5. Finally, the forked arm at the inside end of the torsion bar must be positioned on the splines of the bar so that the bar exerts the correct amount of closing pressure on the valve. To accomplish this, a torque wrench and Honda service tool attachment no. 07039-28302 are absolutely necessary. Fit the torque wrench and attachment

onto the end of the bar and turn the bar in the direction of the arrow stamped on its end until the bolt hole in the bar retaining arm aligns with the bolt hole in the head. The wrench should read 3.7–4.6 ft lbs. If it is outside these limits, partially withdraw the torsion bar while holding the forked arm in position on the valve stem, and rotate the bar in the required direction to position the bolt holes in the retaining arm closer or farther apart as necessary. Recheck the torque wrench reading. Install the retaining bolt in the bar arm when the correct torque is reached.

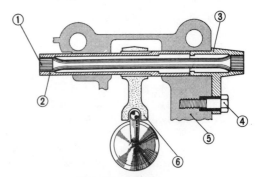

1. Torsion bar splines
2. Torsion bar housing
3. Torsion bar holder arm
4. Holder retaining bolt
5. Cylinder head
6. Torsion bar outer (forked) arm

CAM CHAIN GUIDE ROLLERS

Inspect the rollers for damage and excessive wear. The rollers can be removed after the pins and bracket bolts have been taken out. To install the rollers, assemble rollers A, C, and R in that order. (See the illustration.) Liberally oil them and check for smooth operation after installation.

Measuring the cylinder bore with a dial indicator (1).

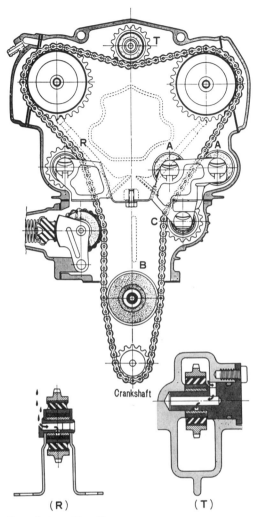

(R)   (T)

Crankshaft

Cam chain guide rollers.

CYLINDER BORE AND PISTONS

Measure the cylinder bore diameter at the top, center, and bottom of the cylinders in both the fore-and-aft and side-to-side directions. If any measurement exceeds 2.760 in. (70.11 mm), or if bore taper or ovality is greater than 0.002 in. (0.05 mm), the cylinders should be rebored. See the specifications at the end of the chapter for piston oversizes. The cylinders should be honed after boring or whenever new rings are to be used.

Measure the diameter of the piston skirt, perpendicular to the wrist pin. Pistons should be replaced when less than 2.751 in. (69.88 mm), or if they are scored or damaged in any way. The piston wrist pin hole should be measured at both ends and 90° apart, and the diameter should be no

greater than 0.6732 in. (17.10 mm). The wrist pin should be a hand press-fit in the piston and connecting rod.

If the original pistons are to be reused, remove the rings and clean the grooves using a piece of one of the old rings. Remove the carbon deposit from the tops of the pistons. Roll the new rings around the grooves before installing them to ensure that there is sufficient clearance. The rings should roll smoothly without binding. Install the rings on the pistons using a ring expander, if possible, to avoid breaking them. Make sure that the mark on the rings is facing up when installed.

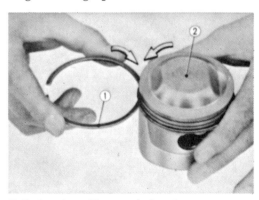

Roll the rings (1) around the piston grooves to check for binding.

Piston and Cylinder Barrel Installation

1. Install the pistons on the connecting rods in their original positions. Be sure to use new wrist pin circlips.

2. Stagger the rings so that the gaps are 120° apart and not in line with, or perpendicular to, the piston boss axis.

3. Install the O-rings on the base of the cylinder barrel and check to make sure

After installing the wrist pin circlips (1), shift the cut portion of the clip from the cut portion of the groove.

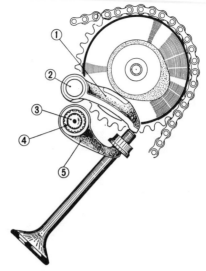

1. Cam follower
2. Cam follower shaft
3. Torsion bar
4. Torsion bar housing
5. Forked arm

that the dowel pins on the crankcase are in place.

4. Fit piston bases, or blocks of wood cut to suitable size, under the pistons to hold them in position. Compress the rings (after oiling them liberally) and carefully install the cylinder barrel over them. Take care not to damage the rings.

5. Before seating the cylinder fully, raise the cam chain through the center and secure the ends so it won't drop back down.

Cylinder Head Installation

1. Install the camshafts and cam followers in the following manner:

Intake side:

Assemble the cam followers onto their eccentric shafts. Position the shaft so that it is in approximately the same position as shown in the accompanying illustration.

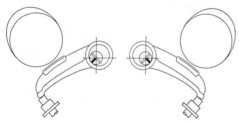

Position the cam follower shafts so that the index mark points away from the center of the cylinder head.

Install the intake camshaft in the head so that the end with the oil line fitting is on the right side. Install the left and right cylinder head side-covers. Check to make sure that the cam rotates freely. Temporarily tighten the cam follower shaft (valve adjuster) locknuts.

Exhaust side:

Assemble the cam followers and shafts into the head, and install the exhaust camshaft. Install the pinion on the tachometer drive. (Don't forget the washer.) Install the tachometer drive, making sure that the pinion is fully seated in the camshaft gear, and then the ignition advance unit and contact breaker plate. Check to make sure that the camshaft rotates freely and temporarily tighten the locknuts.

Tachometer drive pinion (1), washer (2), and gearbox (3).

2. Check the side-clearance of both camshafts. Proper clearance is 0.002–0.014 in. (0.05–0.35 mm). Shims are available for adjusting the side-clearance if this is necessary.

3. Fit the head gasket, stud gaskets, and the three guide pins onto the cylinder.

4. Carefully install the head on the cyl-

Head gasket (1), guide pins (2), and stud gaskets (3).

Aligning the valve timing marks. Camshaft (1) and cam bearing (2), marks aligned (circle).

inder while pulling the cam chain through the center of the head. Take care not to let the chain drop back down.

5. Install the copper washers on the two right-side studs and the flat washers on the remaining six studs.

NOTE: *The two right-side stud holes are oil passageways, and the copper washers must be correctly installed to prevent leaks. The oil flow to the head can be checked by loosening these two stud nuts.*

6. Install the head nuts and tighten them evenly, in the sequence shown, to 20–22 ft lbs.

Cylinder head tightening sequence. Cap nuts (1).

7. To properly set the valve timing, align the mark on the right side of each camshaft to the mark on the right-side cam bearings, as shown. Next, align the "LT" mark on the alternator rotor with the timing index mark on the stator.

8. Connect the ends of the cam chain with a new master link. Take care to prevent the master link from dropping into the engine.

NOTE: *The master link cannot be riv-*

eted where the chain passes over the sprocket.

9. To install the cam chain tensioner, first loosen the locknut and adjuster bolt, push the tensioner roller against the inside of the tensioner, and tighten the adjuster bolt to prevent the roller from popping out. Install the tensioner assembly on the cylinder block.

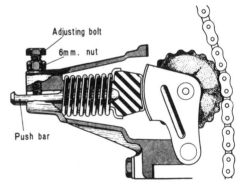

Cross-section of the cam chain tensioner.

10. Reinstall the engine in the frame and perform a complete tune-up, paying special attention to the valve and cam chain adjustments. Refer to chapter three. The valves and cam chain should be checked again after approximately 500 miles have been covered. Don't forget to refill the engine with oil.

SPLITTING THE CRANKCASES

1. Remove the engine from the frame and remove the cylinder head, barrel, and pistons, as described in the previous section.

NOTE: *If desired, the cases can be split without disassembling the top end.*

2. Remove the neutral switch. Take out

the screws and remove the left-side crank-case cover.

3. Unscrew the retaining bolt and re-move the alternator rotor using a rotor puller or a suitably sized bolt.

Removing the alternator rotor (1) with a puller (2).

Starter motor sprocket (1), set plate (2), and starter clutch sprocket (3).

4. Remove the starter clutch sprocket set plate and withdraw the clutch and starter motor sprockets, together with the chain, as an assembly.

5. Remove the kick-start lever. Take out the screws and remove the right-side crankcase cover.

6. Take out the circlip (or bolt on ear-lier models) and remove the oil filter cap. Bend back the locktab, unscrew the nut, and remove the oil filter rotor.

7. Unscrew the clutch pressure plate bolts and remove the pressure plate, discs, and plates.

8. Take out the 29 mm circlip and re-move the clutch hub.

9. Bend back the locktabs and unscrew the oil pump mounting bolts. Remove the oil pump and clutch housing as an assem-bly.

Clutch assembly (1), oil filter (2), and oil pump (3).

Removing the oil filter rotor (1).

Clutch hub (1), circlip (2), and circlip pliers (3).

Removing the clutch housing (1) and oil pump (2).

10. Take out the left circlip and pull out the gearshift spindle. Be careful not to damage the shift drum limit cam plate.

11. Unscrew the four crankcase securing bolts on the upper side and the eleven bolts on the underside. Tap the lower crankcase half with a rubber hammer to break the joint seal and separate the cases.

Assembling the Crankcases

Assembly is a reversal of the disassembly procedures. Observe the following points:

1. Clean the crankcase mating surfaces carefully and inspect them for scratches, signs of leaks, and other damage. Use a sealing compound on the surfaces to prevent oil leaks. Do not get the sealer on the dowel pin holes.

2. Make sure that the kick-starter is properly engaged in the lower crankcase.

3. Handle the starter and alternator cables with care so that the clamps won't be damaged.

4. Tighten the crankcase bolts securely, in an even pattern.

CRANKSHAFT AND CONNECTING RODS

Disassembly

The crankshaft is a built-up unit with one-piece connecting rods and main bearings. It cannot be disassembled and repaired by normal means. Check for excessive wear as described below, and if any of the measurements are beyond the serviceable limits the crankshaft assembly should be replaced.

The crankshaft can be lifted out of the case after the main bearings caps have been unbolted and removed.

Inspection

Use the chart below and the illustrations as a guide to checking the crankshaft components.

Using a dial indicator (1) to check radial clearance of the main bearing (2).

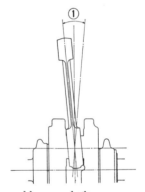

Connecting rod large end tilt measurement (1).

Item		Standard Value	Serviceable Limit
1. Crankshaft run-out °	A, B, C and D	0.002 in. max/0.05 mm	Replace if over 0.008 in./0.2 mm
	E, F and G	0.001 in. max/0.02 mm	Replace if over 0.004 in./0.1 mm
2. Main bearing radial clearance		0.0002–0.0005 in./0.006–0.014 mm	Replace if over 0.001 in./0.03 mm
3. Connecting rod small end		0.6699–0.6706 in./17.016–17.034 mm	Replace if over 0.6721 in./17.07 mm
4. Connecting rod large end radial clearance		0–0.0003 in./0–0.008 mm	Replace if over 0.0020 in./0.05 mm
5. Connecting rod large end side-clearance		0.0028–0.0130 in./0.07–0.33 mm	Replace if over 0.0197 in./0.5 mm
6. Connecting rod large end tilt		0.008–0.04 in./0.2–1.0 mm	Replace if over 0.118 in./3.0 mm

° Run-out equals one-half the dial indicator reading.

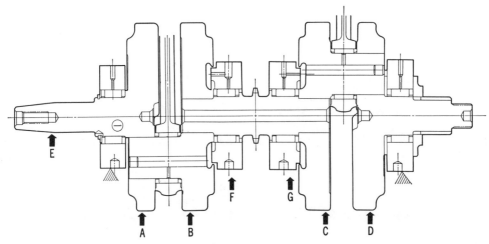

Crankshaft measurement points.

Assembly

When installing the crankshaft into the crankcase make sure that the dowel pin in each crankcase bearing seat is firmly installed, and that the pins fit into the locating holes in the main bearings. Tighten the four center bearing cap bolts gradually and evenly, in a diagonal sequence, to 12–15 ft lbs.

Main bearing locating pins (1).

CLUTCH SERVICE

Disassembly

1. Remove the kick-start lever, take out the retaining screws, and remove the right-side crankcase cover. Refer to the preceding section on splitting the crankcases.

2. Unscrew the clutch pressure plate bolts and withdraw the clutch discs and plates.

3. If you wish to remove the clutch

Removing the clutch plates and discs (1).

housing and hub assembly, first take out the 29 mm circlip and withdraw the clutch hub (center). Next, bend back the locktab and unscrew the oil pump mounting bolts. Remove the oil pump and clutch housing as an assembly.

CAUTION: *Take care not to damage the crankshaft when removing the clutch housing. It may be necessary to remove the oil filter cap and rotor to provide additional clearance.*

Inspection

Measure the thickness of the clutch discs with a vernier caliper or micrometer. Replace the discs if they measure less than 0.122 in. (3.1 mm). Warpage of the plates can be checked by placing them on a flat surface such as a surface plate or a plate of glass, and measuring any gaps with a feeler gauge. Maximum allowable warpage is 0.014 in. (0.35 mm). Measure the free-length of the clutch springs and replace them if less than 1.55 in. (3.94 mm).

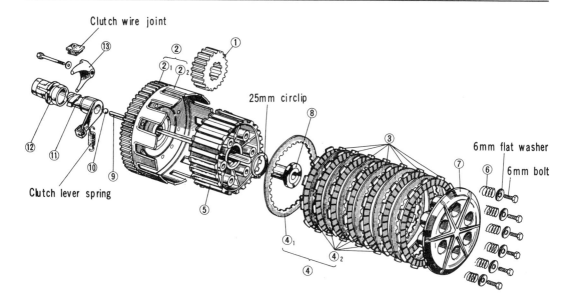

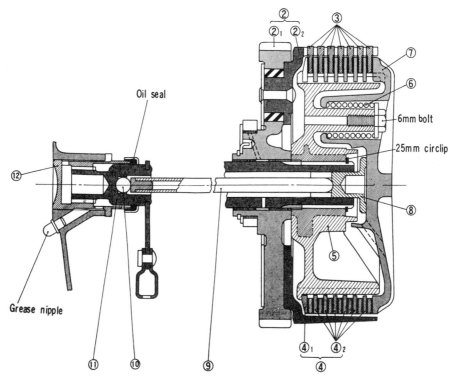

Exploded and sectional views of the clutch assembly.

1. Primary drive gear	4_1. Clutch plate A (1)	9. Release rod
2_1. Clutch housing assembly	4_2. Clutch plate B (6)	10. Steel ball
2_2. Primary driven gear	5. Clutch hub	11. Release spindle
2. Clutch housing	6. Clutch springs	12. Clutch adjuster
3. Clutch discs	7. Pressure plate	13. Adjuster retainer
4. Clutch plates (7)	8. Release rod joint piece	

Examine the primary drive gears at this time for chipping, pitting, and excessive wear, and replace if necessary. Check the radial clearance between the clutch hub and the shaft, and replace the hub if the clearance is greater than 0.0047 in. (0.12 mm). Measure the backlash of the clutch discs in the clutch housing. Replace the housing or discs as necessary if backlash is greater than 0.032 in. (0.8 mm).

Assembly

Assembly is a reversal of the disassembly procedures. Install the discs and plates alternately, beginning with a disc. Take care to torque the pressure plate bolts evenly. Perform a complete clutch adjustment after assembly (refer to chapter two). Observe the following precautions:

1. If the oil pump rod was removed, take care to install it in the correct position. Reversing it will cause pump failure.

2. Use a new oil pump locktab.

3. Before installing the oil pump, make sure that the O-ring is in place. Use a new one if necessary.

4. Take care not to damage the surface of the pressure plate.

TRANSMISSION SERVICE

Disassembly

Remove the engine from the frame and follow disassembly steps 2–11 under "Splitting the Crankcases." Lift out the mainshaft and countershaft assemblies, and refer to the following section for inspection procedures.

Inspection

4-SPEED

1. Measure the diameter of the bearing surfaces at the end of the countershaft and mainshaft. Replace the shafts if the measurement is less than 0.785 in. (19.94 mm).

2. Check the backlash of the C2 and M3 gears on their shafts. Backlash limit is 0.00473 in. (0.12 mm).

3. Measure the backlash of the mating gears with the countershaft and mainshaft assemblies fitted into the case. Maximum acceptable backlash is 0.00826 in. (0.21 mm).

4. Measure the inside diameter of the mainshaft and countershaft bushings, and replace them if the diameter is greater than 0.789 in. (20.06 mm).

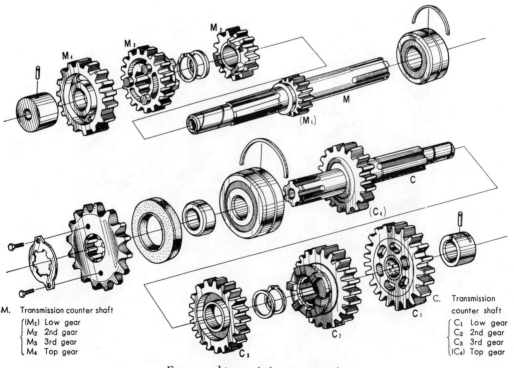

M. Transmission counter shaft
(M_1) Low gear
M_2 2nd gear
M_3 3rd gear
M_4 Top gear

C. Transmission counter shaft
C_1 Low gear
C_2 2nd gear
C_3 3rd gear
(C_4) Top gear

Four-speed transmission components.

5. Replace the C1 gear if its inside diameter is greater than 0.791 in. (20.08 mm).

6. Measure the radial clearance of the ball bearings with a dial indicator. Replace them if the clearance is greater than 0.00197 in. (0.05 mm).

5-Speed

1. Measure the diameter of the mainshaft and countershaft as shown in the accompanying illustration. Replace the shafts if less than 0.785 in. (19.94 mm).

2. Check the backlash of the M2-3, C4, and C5 gears on the splines of their shafts. Maximum acceptable backlash is 0.006 in. (0.15 mm).

3. Measure the backlash of the mating gears with the mainshaft and countershaft assemblies installed in the case. Maximum allowable backlash is 0.006 in. (0.15 mm) (low gear), and 0.008 in. (0.2 mm) (second, third, fourth, and fifth gears).

4. Measure the inside diameter of the mainshaft and countershaft bearings, and replace them if the diameter is greater than 0.789 in. (20.05 mm).

5. Replace the C1 gear if its inside diameter is greater than 0.789 in. (20.05 mm).

6. Measure the radial clearance of the ball bearings with a dial indicator. Replace them if the clearance is greater than 0.002 in. (0.05 mm).

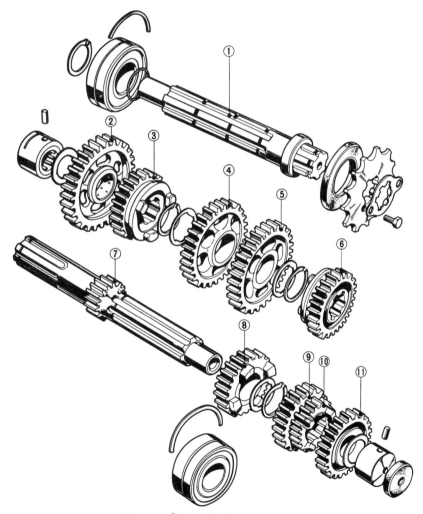

Five-speed transmission components.

1. Countershaft	5. Countershaft second gear	9. 10. Mainshaft second-third gear
2. Countershaft low gear	6. Countershaft top gear	11. Mainshaft top gear
3. Countershaft fourth gear	7. Mainshaft	
4. Countershaft third gear	8. Mainshaft fourth gear	

Assembly

Assemble the transmission components in reverse order of disassembly. Observe the following points:

1. Use only new circlips and make sure that they are properly seated in their grooves.

2. Make sure that the thrust washers are installed on the M2 and C3 gears (four-speed) and the M4, C2, and C3 gears (five-speed).

3. When installing the bearings on the shafts, be sure to install the bearing with the oil groove on the countershaft, and the bearing without the groove on the main-shaft.

4. Check that the bearing set rings and dowel pins are in place before installing the shaft assemblies in the crankcase.

5. Assemble the crankcases as previously described.

SHIFTER MECHANISM

Disassembly

1. Split the crankcases and lift out the transmission mainshaft and countershaft assemblies as previously described.

2. Remove the shift drum stop (four-speed models). Unscrew the bolt and disassemble the neutral limit arm and shift drum stop (five-speed models).

3. Remove the shift fork guide pin clips and pull out the pins. Withdraw the shift drum from the case by lightly tapping in from the neutral switch side.

Inspection

1. Check the shift forks using the chart below as a guide.

2. Measure the width of the tracks in the shift drum. Replace the drum if the width exceeds 0.256 in. (6.5 mm) or if the tracks are damaged.

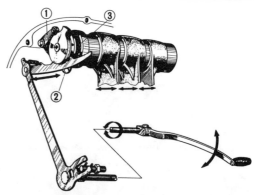

Shifter mechanism. Neutral limit arm (1), shift drum stop (2), and ball bearing (3).

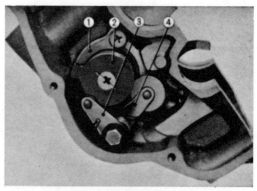

1. Bearing set plate
2. Shift drum
3. Shift drum neutral stop
4. Shift drum stop

Assembly

1. Install the shift drum and forks into the case. Take care not to damage the crankcase oil seal.

2. Install the fork guide pins and pin clips, taking note of the proper clip installation direction.

3. On four-speed models the right shift fork fits around the C2 gear, and the left fork around the M3 gear. On five-speed

Item		Standard Value	Serviceable Limit
Inside Diam.		1.3385–1.339 in./34.0–34.025 mm	Replace if over 1.3425 in./34.1 mm
End thickness	Left Right	0.1941–0.1968 in./4.93–5.0 mm	Replace if under 0.181 in./4.6 mm
	Center	0.2334–0.236 in./5.93–6.0 mm	Replace if under 0.2205 in./5.6 mm
Bend in fork end (left, right)		Within 0.004 in./0.1 mm	Replace if over 0.031 in./0.8 mm

models the left fork is fitted to gear C4, the right fork on gear C5, and the center fork on the M2-3 gear. Install the transmission shaft assemblies in the case.

4. Reassemble the remaining parts in reverse order of disassembly. Check to make sure that the action of the shifter mechanism is smooth.

KICK-START MECHANISM SERVICE

The kick-start shaft and ratchet assembly can be removed after the crankcases have been split. A damaged shaft and pinion assembly should be replaced. when reassembling, always use a new 8 mm lockwasher.

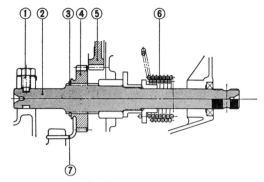

Cross-section of kick-start components.

1. Set bolt
2. Spindle
3. Circlip
4. Pinion
5. Countershaft low gear
6. Spring
7. Friction spring

Engine Specifications

CYLINDER HEAD		125	175	350	450
Valves, Guides, and Springs— valve run-out at face:					
maximum,	in.	0.001	0.001	0.001	0.001
	mm	0.03	0.03	0.03	0.03
valve stem diameter:					
intake (nominal),	in.	0.216	0.216	0.275	0.275
	mm	5.48–5.49	5.48–5.49	6.98–6.99	6.98–6.99
exhaust (nominal),	in.	0.215	0.215	0.274	0.275
	mm	5.46–5.47	5.46–5.47	6.96–6.97	6.97–6.98
valve guide bore:					
nominal,	in.	0.217	0.217	N.A.	0.276
	mm	5.50–5.51	5.50–5.51	N.A.	7.0–7.01
maximum,	in.	0.219	0.219	N.A.	0.278
	mm	5.55	5.55	N.A.	7.05
stem-to-guide clearance:					
intake (nominal),	in.	N.A.	N.A.	0.001	0.001
	mm	N.A.	N.A.	0.01–0.03	0.01–0.03
(maximum),	in.	0.003	0.003	0.003	0.003
	mm	0.08	0.08	0.08	0.08
exhaust (nominal),	in.	N.A.	N.A.	0.002	0.002
	mm	N.A.	N.A.	0.03–0.05	0.03–0.05
(maximum),	in.	0.004	0.004	0.0035	0.004
	mm	0.10	0.10	0.09	0.10
spring free-length:					
inner (nominal),	in.	1.028	1.189	1.567	——
	mm	26.1	30.2	39.8	——
(minimum),	in.	1.008	1.169	1.547	——
	mm	25.6	29.7	39.3	——
outer (nominal),	in.	1.264	1.252	1.929	——
	mm	32.1	31.8	49.0	——
(minimum),	in.	1.221	1.205	1.882	——
	mm	31.0	30.6	47.8	——

Engine Specifications

		125	175	350	450
CYLINDER HEAD					
Camshaft and Rocker Arms—					
valve timing: (deg):					
intake opens (BTDC)		5°	10°	①	10°
intake closes (ABDC)		30°	40°	①	40°
exhaust opens (BBDC)		5°	40°	①	40°
exhaust closes (ATDC)		35°	10°	①	10°
cam height:					
intake (nominal),	in.	1.031	0.987	1.452	③
	mm	26.18	25.06	36.88	
exhaust (nominal),	in.	1.013	0.979	1.452	③
	mm	25.74	24.87	36.88	
intake (minimum),	in.	1.024	N.A.	1.444	③
	mm	26.0	N.A.	36.68	
exhaust (minimum),	in.	1.008	N.A.	1.444	③
	mm	25.6	N.A.	36.68	
base circle diameter:					
nominal,	in.	0.827	0.827	N.A.	N.A.
	mm	21.0	21.0	N.A.	N.A.
minimum,	in.	N.A.	N.A.	N.A.	N.A.
	mm	N.A.	N.A.	N.A.	N.A.
side clearance:	in.	N.A.	N.A.	0.008–0.024	0.002–0.014
	mm	N.A.	N.A.	0.2–0.6	0.05–0.35
camshaft end diameter:					
minimum,	in.	1.296	0.785	0.862 ②	0.862
(left)	mm	32.91	19.94	21.92	21.92
minimum,	in.	0.785	0.785	0.862 ②	0.862
(right)	mm	19.94	19.94	21.92	21.92
rocker arm shaft clearance:					
nominal,	in.	0.001	0.001	N.A.	④
	mm	0.02–0.04	0.02–0.04	N.A.	
maximum,	in.	0.003	0.003	N.A.	④
	mm	0.08	0.08	N.A.	
rocker arm shaft diameter:					
nominal,	in.	0.393	0.393	0.510	⑤
	mm	9.98	9.98	12.950	
maximum,	in.	0.390	0.390	0.508	⑤
	mm	9.92	9.92	12.9	

① Serial numbers prior to CB/CL 350E-1045164—10° BTDC, 35° ATDC, 30° BBDC, 10° ABDC; serial numbers after CB/CL 350E-1045165—5° BTDC, 30° ATDC, 30° BBDC, 5° ABDC; SL 350K1 and K2—TDC, 20° ABDC, 25° BBDC, TDC.
② End cover (cam bearing) inside diameter, maximum—0.868 in. (20.05 mm).
③ Cam lift, intake and exhaust—nominal: 0.185 in. (4.70 mm);
　　　　　　　　　　　　　　　 minimum: 0.183 in. (4.65 mm).
④ Cam follower bearing diameter—maximum: 0.405 in. (10.28 mm).
⑤ Cam follower shaft journal diameter—minimum: 0.398 in. (10.10 mm).

		125	175	350	450
CYLINDERS, PISTONS, AND RINGS					
Cylinder Bore—					
nominal,	in.	1.732	2.030	2.520	2.756
	mm	44.0	52.00	64.01	70.0
maximum,	in.	1.736	2.051	2.524	2.760
	mm	44.1	52.1	64.1	70.11
taper and ovality:					
maximum,	in.	0.002	0.002	0.002	0.002
	mm	0.05	0.05	0.05	0.05

Engine Specifications

		125	175	350	450
CYLINDERS, PISTONS, AND RINGS					
Pistons—					
diameter:					
nominal,	in.	1.732	2.046	2.519	2.754
	mm	43.96	51.96	63.97	69.95
minimum,	in.	1.728	①	2.510	2.751
	mm	43.9		63.9	69.88
wrist pin hole diameter:					
nominal,	in.	0.512	0.551–0.552	0.591	0.669
	mm	13.00	14.00	15.00	17.00
maximum:	in.	0.513	0.553	0.594	0.673
	mm	13.05	14.05	15.08	17.1
wrist pin diameter:					
nominal,	in.	N.A.	N.A.	0.590	0.669
	mm	N.A.	N.A.	14.99	16.99
minimum,	in.	N.A.	N.A.	0.589	0.667
	mm	N.A.	N.A.	14.96	16.95
available oversizes:	mm	(3) 44.25–44.75	(4) 52.25–53.00	(4) 64.25–65.00	(4) 70.25–71.00
Rings—					
end gap:					
compression (nominal),	in.	0.006–0.014	0.006–0.016	0.008–0.016	0.012–0.03
	mm	0.15–0.35	0.15–0.40	0.2–0.4	0.3–0.5
oil control (nominal),	in.	0.006–0.015	0.006–0.016	0.008–0.016	0.008–0.016
	mm	0.15–0.40	0.15–0.40	0.2–0.4	0.2–0.4
compression (maximum),	in.	0.032	0.032	0.032	0.032
	mm	0.8	0.8	0.8	0.08
oil control (maximum),	in.	0.032	0.032	0.032	0.032
	mm	0.8	0.8	0.8	0.8
side clearance:					
top (nominal),	in.	0.001	0.001–0.002	0.001–0.002	0.002–0.003
	mm	0.03	0.03–0.05	0.03–0.05	0.04–0.07
2nd (nominal),	in.	0.001	0.001	0.001	0.001–0.002
	mm	0.03	0.02–0.04	0.02–0.04	0.02–0.04
oil (nominal),	in.	0.001	0.001	0.001	0.001
	mm	0.03	0.02–0.04	0.02–0.04	0.01
top (maximum),	in.	0.004	0.004	0.007	0.006
	mm	0.01	0.01	0.18	0.15
2nd (maximum),	in.	0.004	0.004	0.006	0.006
	mm	0.01	0.01	0.17	0.15
oil (maximum),	in.	0.004	0.004	0.006	0.004
	mm	0.01	0.01	0.17	0.1

① Piston-to-cylinder clearance, maximum—0.004 in. (0.1 mm).

		125	175	350	450
CRANKSHAFT AND CONNECTING RODS					
Crankshaft run-out—					
shaft end:					
nominal,	in.	0.001	0.001	0.001	0.001
	mm	0.02	0.02	0.02	0.02
maximum,	in.	0.003	0.003	0.006	0.004
	mm	0.08	0.08	0.15	0.10
counterweight:					
nominal,	in.	N.A.	N.A.	0.004	0.002
	mm	N.A.	N.A.	0.10	0.05
maximum,	in.	N.A.	N.A.	0.012	0.008
	mm	N.A.	N.A.	0.30	0.20

Engine Specifications

		125	175	350	450
CRANKSHAFT AND CONNECTING RODS					
Main bearing radial clearance—					
nominal,	in.	0.002	0.002	0.001	0.0005
	mm	0.05	0.05	0.02	0.014
maximum,	in.	0.004	0.004	0.002	0.001
	mm	0.1	0.01	0.05	0.03
Con rod bearing radial clearance—					
nominal,	in.	N.A.	N.A.	0.0005	0.0003
	mm	N.A.	N.A.	0.012	0.008
maximum,	in.	0.004	0.004	0.002	0.002
	mm	0.1	0.01	0.05	0.05
Con rod side clearance—					
nominal,	in.	①	②	0.003–0.013	0.003–0.013
	mm			0.07–0.33	0.07–0.33
maximum,	in.	①	②	0.023	0.020
	mm			0.60	0.50
Wrist pin bushing diameter—					
nominal,	in.	N.A.	N.A.	0.592	0.670
	mm	N.A.	N.A.	15.03	17.03
maximum,	in.	N.A.	N.A.	0.593	0.672
	mm	N.A.	N.A.	15.07	17.07

① Main bearing side clearance, nominal—0.002 in. (0.05 mm); maximum—0.004 in. (0.1 mm).
② Main bearing side clearance, nominal—0.001 in. (0.02 mm); maximum—0.002 in. (0.05).

5 · Lubrication Systems

Operational Description

All twin-cylinder Hondas utilize a plunger type oil pump driven from the clutch outer housing. Oil picked up from the crankcase sump is first routed through the centrifugal oil filter before it is pressure-fed to the crankshaft assembly and cylinder head components. All other engine and transmission parts are lubricated by oil splash. A small filter screen is fitted at the oil pump pick-up to block any large impurities in the sump from being pulled through the oil pump. The screen does not require cleaning until the engine is disassembled for overhaul.

Oil pump failure on these models is rare, and if the oil is changed regularly and the centrifugal filter cleaned now and then, you should experience no trouble with the pump for the life of the engine.

Oil Pump Service—All Models

REMOVAL AND INSTALLATION

To remove the oil pump it is necessary to remove the clutch unit. Refer to chapter four. The oil pump and clutch are unbolted and removed together.

DISASSEMBLY

1. Remove the circlip and separate the pump rod from the clutch housing. The plunger can be removed from the pump rod after the pin is driven out.

2. The pressure relief valve and check valve balls and springs can be removed from the pump after the retaining caps have been unscrewed.

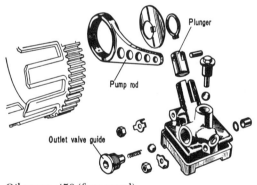

Oil pump, 450 (four-speed).

INSPECTION

Examine the plunger bore in the oil pump housing for scoring or other damage. Measure the diameter of the bore and plunger at four points: two points 90° apart at top and bottom. Compare the dimensions obtained with the specifications at the end of the chapter and replace parts as necessary.

Inspect the pressure relief valve balls

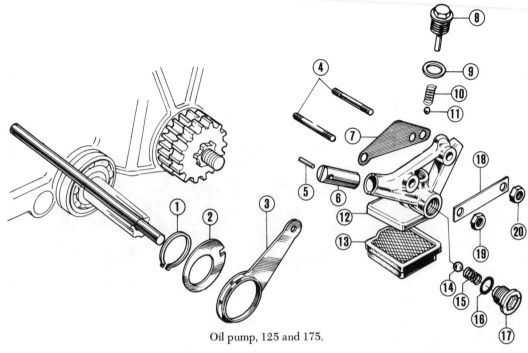

Oil pump, 125 and 175.

1. Circlip	8. Suction valve bolt	15. Valve spring
2. Pump rod side washer	9. Suction valve bolt packing	16. O-ring
3. Pump rod	10. Suction valve spring	17. Outlet valve guide
4. Stud	11. $\frac{5}{16}$ in. steel ball	18. Pump lockwasher
5. Plunger pump pin	12. Oil pump body	19. 20. 6 mm hex nut
6. Plunger	13. Pump filter screen	
7. Pump body gasket	14. $\frac{5}{16}$ in. steel ball	

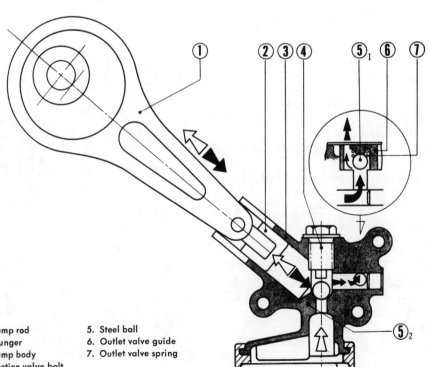

1. Pump rod	5. Steel ball
2. Plunger	6. Outlet valve guide
3. Pump body	7. Outlet valve spring
4. Suction valve bolt	

Oil pump, 350.

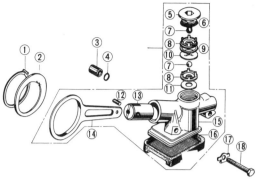

Oil pump, 450 (five-speed).

1. Circlip
2. Pump rod side washer
3. Knock pin
4. O-ring
5. Oil pump ball stopper bolt
6. O-ring
7. Steel ball
8. Oil pump ball seat
9. Rubber ring
10. Oil pump ball stopper
11. Rubber seat
12. Oil pump plunger pin
13. Pump plunger
14. Pump rod
15. Oil pump body
16. Filter screen
17. Lockwasher
18. Bolt

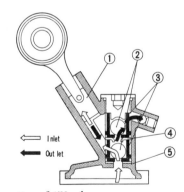

Cross-section of 450 oil pump.

1. Plunger
2. Steel ball
3. Ball seat
4. Ball stopper
5. Rubber seat

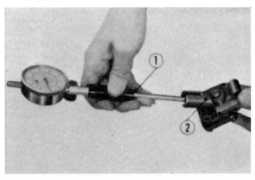

Using a dial indicator (1) to measure the pump body bore (2).

Using a micrometer (1) to measure the plunger diameter (2).

and ball seats for damage and wear. The complete pump assembly should be replaced if the valve balls show extensive wear.

ASSEMBLY

Assemble the oil pump in reverse order of disassembly. Make sure that all components have been cleaned thoroughly and coated with fresh engine oil. Note the following points:

1. Do not overtighten the check valve and pressure relief valve caps.

2. The pump rod retaining circlip is a special type and should not be substituted for with any others.

3. Take care to install the pump rod in the correct position. Reversing it will cause pump failure.

4. Use new O-rings and make sure they are correctly positioned. Refer to the accompanying illustrations.

5. Use a new locktab under the mounting nuts when installing the pump.

Oil Pump Specifications

125 and 175

Plunger-to-housing calculated clearance:	
nominal—in.	0.001–0.0025
mm	0.025–0.063
maximum—in.	0.0067
mm	0.17
Oil pump capacity:	
nominal—cc/min @ rpm	3,600 @ 10,000
minimum—cc/min @ rpm	3,400 @ 10,000

350

Bore diameter:	
nominal—in.	0.630–0.631
mm	16.000–16.018
maximum—in.	0.634
mm	16.10
Plunger diameter:	
nominal—in.	0.628–0.629
mm	15.955–15.970
minimum—in.	0.627
mm	15.930

450

Plunger-to-housing calculated clearance:	
nominal—in.	0.001–0.0025
mm	0.025–0.063
maximum—in.	0.0067
mm	0.017

6 · Fuel Systems

Description and Operation

Two types of carburetors are used on the Honda twins: the conventional direct-control slide type carburetors, used primarily on the 125 and 175, and the constant velocity (CV) type, used primarily on the 350 and 450. The different types can be easily identified by the throttle cable connection. In the direct-control type carburetor, the throttle cable enters the carburetor top, while in the CV carburetor, the throttle cable connects to a lever at the side. Both types are manufactured by Keihin.

DIRECT-CONTROL TYPE CARBURETOR

These carburetors are quite conventional in design and operation, and have been used for many years on almost all Hondas. The throttle twist-grip is connected to, and directly controls, the throttle slide; different slide openings vary the size of the carburetor venturi. After air is drawn into the carburetor and past the slide, it enters a relatively low-pressure area and, in doing so, draws fuel up past the jet needle. In this way the proper air/fuel mixture is created, due to the relationship between the intake manifold vacuum and air velocity through the carburetor. The size of the jet and the taper of the jet needle determine how much fuel is drawn for a given amount of vacuum and air velocity.

It can be seen here that if the throttle is opened suddenly (yanking the slide up just as quickly) at low engine rpm, air velocity through the venturi will be low because of the low intake vacuum and large throttle (venturi) opening, and an insufficient amount of fuel will be drawn for the volume of air inducted. This creates a momentary lean mixture condition and causes a hesitation before the engine accelerates cleanly. It can also be seen that lowering or raising the jet needle position relative to the slide or changing the main jet size will have an effect on mixture strength. Changing the position of the needle or changing the needle taper will affect running at mid-range throttle openings (from about $1/4$–$3/4$ throttle) and changing the main jet size will affect full throttle running. This is so because at small throttle openings the needle effectively plugs the jet tube completely and the low-speed system takes over, while at full throttle, the needle is withdrawn from the jet tube enough that the main jet is virtually unrestricted.

Low-Speed System

At small throttle openings (approximately $1/4$–$1/8$ throttle), the carburetor low-speed system takes over. Air entering the carburetor is regulated by the air screw, after which it enters the low-speed jet bleed hole. The air then mixes with the fuel entering the low-speed jet and the mixture is then discharged from the pilot outlet under the slide. The mixture is then carried into the engine along with the small amount of air allowed to pass through the slight opening or cutaway of the slide. As the slide is raised past ¼ throttle opening, the relatively small amount of mixture discharged by the low-speed jet is overshadowed by the volume of air now being allowed to enter, and, of course, the main jet system is coming into play as the needle is withdrawn from the jet tube. At the same time, increased air flow and vacuum (bypassing the air screw), and increased pressure through the venturi (over the low-speed jet discharge outlet) effectively closes off the low-speed system and the transition to the main system is complete.

Float Chamber

In order to maintain the correct flow of fuel to the carburetor jets at all engine speeds and throttle openings, a sufficient amount of fuel under relatively constant delivery pressure must be available. The float chamber serves to accomplish this. Fuel entering the float chamber from the fuel tank must pass between the float needle and seat valve. As fuel fills the chamber, the float rises with the fuel level and when a preset level is reached, the float shuts off flow by pressing the needle against the seat, closing the valve. As fuel is consumed and the level drops, the float will have followed the level, allowing more fuel to enter so that a constant level will be maintained.

It is very important that the float level be correctly set so that the proper mixture strength is maintained. An adjustable float level gauge, suitable for most motorcycle carburetors, is available from Honda dealers (part number 07144-99998). An improperly set float level can cause poor or erratic performance in both the low and high-speed ranges.

CONSTANT VELOCITY CARBURETOR

The constant velocity carburetor is basically the same as the direct-control type carburetor, except that the throttle twist-grip is not connected directly to the throttle slide. Instead, in the CV carburetor, the throttle grip and cable are connected to a butterfly valve located between the intake manifold and throttle slide. As the throttle butterfly is opened, the manifold vacuum evacuates air from the top of the slide chamber through a passage in the slide. Consequently, on demand from the engine the slide is raised and more air is admitted, and the tapered jet needle is proportionally lifted out of the jet tube to admit more fuel.

The term "constant velocity" (or constant vacuum) refers to the speed of the air passing over the main jet tube and the vacuum in the carburetor throat (between the butterfly and slide), which remains constant due to the movement of the piston in relation to the vacuum. As the engine demands more air and the manifold vacuum increases, the slide responds by lifting in proportion to the vacuum. Thus the carburetor air speed and vacuum remain constant, because an increase in vacuum means an increase in slide lift, which in turn increases the amount of air passing through the carburetor by altering the size of the air passage (venturi), and compensating for the increased engine demands with a larger flow of air. A constant vacuum indicates a constant velocity, and vice versa.

The advantages of the constant velocity carburetor are good fuel economy, smooth throttle response, and steady performance throughout the entire rpm range.

Fuel Tap—All Models

REMOVAL, CLEANING, AND INSPECTION

1. Turn the tap to "stop" and disconnect the lines.
2. Raise the seat, and raise and support the rear of the fuel tank.
3. Unscrew the cup from the tap, and remove the O-ring and filter strainer.
4. Remove the two mounting screws and the fuel tap.
5. Remove the two screws from the lever retaining plate and remove the plate, O-ring, and gasket.

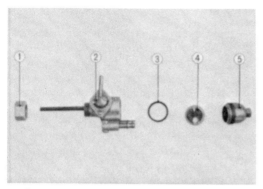

Fuel tap components.

1. Securing nut
2. Fuel top body
3. Gasket
4. Filter screen
5. Cup

6. Clean all components in solvent and dry thoroughly. Inspect for wear and cracks.

7. Assemble the tap in reverse order of disassembly, using new gaskets and O-rings.

8. Install the fuel tap on the tank and check for proper fuel flow. (Catch the gasoline in a can or jar.)

9. Lower the tank, install the fuel lines, and check for leaks.

Fuel Tank—All Models

REMOVAL AND INSTALLATION

1. Turn the fuel tap to "stop" and disconnect the fuel lines.

2. Raise the seat. On early 125s and 175s it will be necessary to loosen the two seat mounting bolts and remove the seat.

3. Lift the rear of the fuel tank out of the rubber mount and withdraw the tank up and toward the rear of the machine, taking care not to snag any cables or wiring on the mounting flanges.

NOTE: *On early 450s the rear of the tank is retained by a bolt and rubber bushings.*

Installation is in reverse order of removal. Be careful not to accidentally strain or reroute any cables when positioning the tank. Make sure that the fuel lines are secured properly at the fuel tap.

Carburetor Overhaul

DIRECT-CONTROL TYPE

Removal and Installation

1. Turn the fuel tap off and disconnect the fuel line.

2. Unscrew the cap from the top of the carburetor and carefully withdraw the slide.

3. Loosen and slide back the air filter connecting clamp at the carburetor.

4. Disconnect one side of the choke linkage rod (twin carburetors).

5. Unbolt and remove the carburetor from the cylinder head.

Installation is in reverse order of removal. The following points should be noted:

1. When reinstalling the slide in the carburetor, take special care not to damage the needle when dropping it into the jet tube. The tab in the slide bore must engage the slot in the slide. Tighten the cap firmly by hand after the slide has been installed.

2. Check carburetor adjustment and synchronization after installation, and check for smooth throttle operation. Refer to chapter three.

Disassembly

1. Disconnect the carburetor slide from the throttle cable by compressing the spring and feeding the inner cable into the slide so that the cable end can be disengaged from the retaining slot.

2. Release the float bowl by swivelling back the retaining clip. Try to hold the carburetor in its normal position so that the gasoline in the float bowl will not be spilled.

3. Tap out the float hinge pin using a small diameter rod or drift. Remove the float and lift the float valve needle out of the valve seat. Unscrew the valve seat from the carburetor body.

4. Using a small screwdriver, remove the main jet, low-speed jet, throttle stop screw, and air screw.

5. Unscrew the main jet tube, using the correct size wrench.

Cleaning

Clean all components in solvent or carburetor cleaner and dry thoroughly with

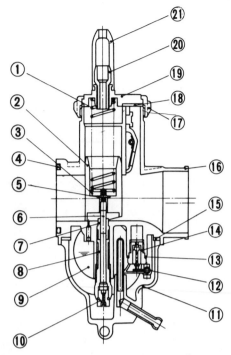

Cross-section of a direct control type carburetor.

1. Coil spring
2. Throttle slide
3. Needle clip plate
4. O-ring
5. Bar clip
6. Jet needle
7. Needle jet
8. Needle jet holder
9. Float
10. Main jet
11. Float chamber body

12. Arm pin
13. Valve seat
14. Slow jet
15. Float chamber washer
16. Body
17. Cap
18. Top washer
19. Top
20. Cable adjuster
21. Rubber cap

compressed air. If an acid type carburetor cleaner is used, do not clean the float or any rubber or plastic parts in it.

Inspection

1. Make sure that the surface of the throttle slide is clean and smooth. Light scoring can be smoothed with fine emery cloth.

2. Examine the jet needle for wear as indicated by bright spots or uneven taper. If wear is noticeable replace both the needle and the needle jet tube.

3. Examine the float valve needle for wear. If replacement is necessary, replace the needle and seat as a unit.

4. Inspect the carburetor body for cracks.

Assembly

Assemble in reverse order of disassembly. Observe the following points:

1. Use new gaskets and O-rings.

2. The float level must be checked and adjusted if necessary. The float should be positioned so that when the float arm just touches the tip of the float needle, the distance from the the top of the float to the float bowl mating surface on the carburetor is as close as possible to the specification given at the end of the chapter for your carburetor.

3. Do not overtighten the jets when installing them in the carburetor body.

4. Make sure that the jet needle is installed in the same position as when removed. Changing the needle position in the slide will affect running at mid-range throttle openings.

5. After installing the carburetor check for smooth operation of the choke. On twin carburetor installations, check to make sure that the clearance between the choke valve and throttle bore is less than 0.02 in. (0.5 mm) and that both chokes operate simultaneously. Adjust with the linkage rod if necessary.

CONSTANT VELOCITY TYPE

Removal and Installation

1. Turn the fuel tap off and disconnect the fuel line.

2. Disconnect the throttle cable from the linkage at the carburetor.

3. Loosen the air filter connecting clamp at the carburetor and loosen or remove the air filter housing so that the carburetor can be moved back slightly.

4. Loosen the carburetor-to-intake tube mounting clamp and remove the carburetor.

Installation is in reverse order of removal. The following points should be noted:

1. Make sure that the carburetor is securely clamped to the intake tube. If necessary, use a new clamp.

2. Check carburetor adjustment and synchronization after installation. (Refer to chapter three.) Check for smooth throttle operation.

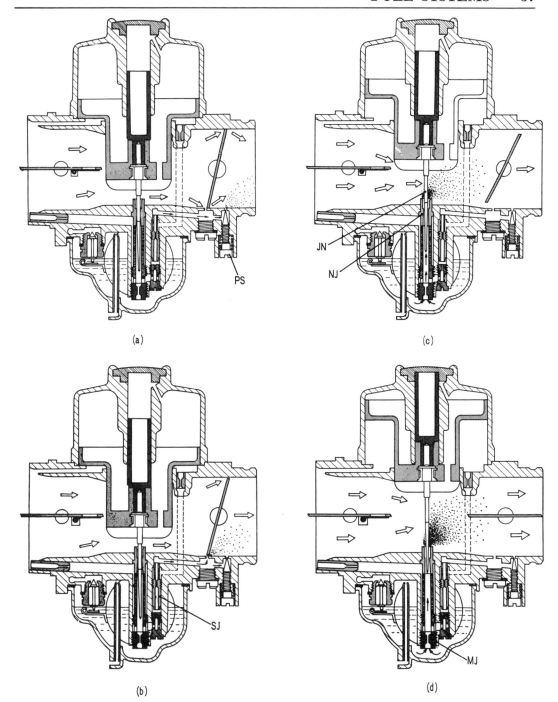

(a)　　　(c)

(b)　　　(d)

Operation of a constant velocity carburetor at various throttle openings (450 shown).

Disassembly, Cleaning, Inspection, and Assembly

Refer to the preceding section on direct-control type carburetors, as the procedures are nearly identical. In the "disas-

sembly" section, omit step one and substitute the following:

1. Remove the carburetor top and lift out the slide. Take care not to damage the slide diaphragm (350 only).

Carburetor Specifications

	CB 125	CL 125	CD 125	CB 175	CL 175
Type	(2) Keihin	(2) Keihin	(1) Keihin CV	(2) Keihin	(2) Keihin
Bore diameter (mm)	18	18	——	20	22
Main jet (no.)	92	92	——	95	98
Low-speed jet (no.)	35	35	——	35	38
Slide cutaway (no.)	2.0	2.0	——	2.0	3.0
Jet needle	18231	18234	——	3°, 2.535	4°, 2.535
	(2 stage)	(2 stage)		(3 stage)	(3 stage)
Air screw openings *	1⅛ ± ¼	1⅛ ± ¼	——	1⅛ ± ¼	1⅛ ± ¼
Air jet (no.)	150	150	——	100	100
Float height (mm)	21	21	——	19.5	28.0

* Number of turns from fully closed.

	CD 175	SL 175	CB/CL 350 †	CB/CL 350 ‡	CB/CL 350 § SL 350 (1970)	SL 350K1 & K2
Type		(2) Keihin	(2) Keihin CV	(2) Keihin CV	(2) Keihin CV	(2) Keihin
Bore diameter (mm)	——	——	28	28	28	24
Main jet (no.)	——	——	60/115	70/110	70/105	120
			(pri/sec)	(pri/sec)	(pri/sec)	
Low-speed jet (no.)	——	——	38	35	35	40
Slide cutaway (no.)	——	——	12°, 1.0	12°, 1.0	12°, 1.0	2.5 x 1.8 x 0.2
Jet needle	——	——	3°30', 2.595	3°30', 2.595	3°30', 2.595	3°, 2.515
Air screw opening *	——	——	¾ ± ⅛	1.0 ± ⅛	¾ ± ⅛	1.0 ± ¼
Air jet (no.)	——	——	50/50	150/50	150/50	150
			(pri/sec)	(pri/sec)	(pri/sec)	
Float height (mm)	——	——	19	21	26	25

* Number of turns from fully closed.
† Up to engine number E-1045165.
‡ From engine number E-1045165 to E-1065279.
§ From engine number E-1065279 to present.

	CB 450 (4-speed)	CB/CL 450 (5-speed)
Type	(2) Keihin CV	(2) Keihin CV
Bore diameter (mm)	36	36
Main jet (no.)	125	130
Low-speed jet (no.)	38	38
Slide cutaway (no.)	14°, 1.0	14°, 0.9
Jet needle	2°26', 2.275	3°, 2.275
Air screw opening *	¾ ± ¼	1.0 ± ¼
Air jet (no.)	50	50
Float height (mm)	20	20

* Number of turns from fully closed.

7 · Electrical Systems

Charging System—All Models

The charging system consists of the alternator, battery, rectifier, and, on some models, a voltage regulator.

The alternator consists basically of six-pole stator and rotor, which is bolted to the end of the crankshaft. Electrical current is induced in the stator as the rotor cuts across the magnetic field of the stator magnets. The advantages of an alternator over a DC generator is that it is less bulky and has fewer moving parts, and it produces a larger voltage at low speeds.

Since an alternator produces alternating current and the battery requires direct current for recharging, it is necessary to employ some means of converting the AC to DC. The selenium rectifier serves to accomplish this by allowing the alternating current produced by the alternator to pass through it in one direction only, thus converting it before it reaches the battery.

On the 125s and 175s, alternator output is balanced against the normal electrical needs of the machine, and a voltage regulator is not used on these models. The alternator is matched to the electrical system so that during day running (lights off) the battery will be receiving a normal charge, and during night running, the battery,

with the additional load, will (hopefully) be receiving enough current to keep it from discharging. Frequent battery maintenance may be necessary if your bike is used almost exclusively for either day or night riding, or other abnormal conditions.

350s and 5-speed 450s are equipped with a silicon type voltage regulator which is non-mechanical and cannot be adjusted. With the addition of the regulator, a higher capacity alternator, which is capable of supplying a strong charge at full electrical load, is also used. As long as battery voltage is within the normal range, the regulator does not function, and the alternator supplies its total output to the battery. When normal battery voltage is exceeded and the battery is being overcharged, the regulator functions to ground the excessive current and maintain a normal charging rate.

If a charging system fault is suspected, the first thing to do is check the overload fuse located near the battery. If it is not burned out, inspect the wires and connections at the battery, alternator, rectifier, and regulator (if applicable). Make sure that the rectifier is securely mounted to the frame. If any defects are found, alternator output should be checked (after the fault is corrected) to ensure that the alternator and rectifier have not been damaged by being inadvertently disconnected from the circuit. If no obvious fault can be found in the charging system, refer to the following sections for testing and repair procedures.

ALTERNATOR OUTPUT TEST

125 and 175

1. Check the state of charge of the battery. (Refer to chapter two.) If necessary, recharge the battery before proceeding with the test.

2. Connect an ammeter between the positive (+) battery terminal and the input (alternator) side of the rectifier. Start the engine and compare the readings obtained with those in the table.

3. If alternator output is insufficient, the fault lies either in the wiring between the alternator and rectifier or in the alternator itself. Check the wiring and refer to the "ALTERNATOR SERVICE" section. If the alternator is producing a sufficient amount of current, it can be assumed that either the rectifier or the wiring between the rectifier and battery is at fault.

NOTE: *Remember that these models do not have a regulator, and running constantly with the lights on or under other heavy electrical load can cause slow battery discharge, which should be considered normal.*

350 and 450

1. Check the state of charge of the battery. (Refer to chapter two.) If necessary, recharge the battery before proceeding with the test.

2. Connect the positive lead of an ammeter to the yellow alternator lead and ground the negative lead on the engine. Start the engine and run it at a steady 5,000 rpm. The ammeter should read 1.5–2.5 amps (350) or 4.0–5.0 amps (450). Excessive amperage indicates a bad regulator.

3. Next, switch the ammeter lead from the yellow wire to the white alternator wire. Start the engine, turn the headlight on (high beam), and run it at 5,000 rpm. The ammeter should read approximately the same as before, 1.5–2.5 amps (350) or 4.0–5.0 amps (450). Battery voltage at 5,000 rpm in either case should be 14.8 volts.

4. If output in steps two and three is sufficient, chances are that the rectifier or wiring between the rectifier and battery is at fault.

5. If alternator output in steps two and three is insufficient, disconnect the yellow wire from the regulator, making sure it does not touch ground, and check the output again at 5,000 rpm with the lights on. If a good reading is obtained, the regulator is at fault (assuming there are no breaks in the wiring). If output is still insufficient, the problem lies in the alternator itself.

TESTING THE RECTIFIER— ALL MODELS

If alternator output is satisfactory but the battery discharges as the engine is run-

Alternator Output Table, 125 and 175

Model	Item	Charging Start	Charging Current /3,000 rpm	Charging Current /5,000 rpm	Charging Current /10,000 rpm
CB 175	Daytime	Max 2,400 rpm	——	Min 0.5 A	Max 3.0 A
	Nighttime	Max 2,800 rpm	——	Min 0.5 A	Max 3.0 A
	Battery voltage	12.3 V	——	13 V	16.5 V
CL 175	Daytime	Max 2,400 rpm	——	Min 0.5 A	Max 3.0 A
	Nighttime	Max 2,800 rpm	——	Min 0.5 A	Max 3.0 A
	Battery voltage	13.2 V	——	14 V	16.5 V
CB 125	Daytime	Max 1,300 rpm	Min 2.0 A	Min 2.7 A	Max 4.5 A
	Nighttime	Max 1,900 rpm	Min 1.2 A	Min 2.0 A	Max 4.0 A
	Battery voltage	6.3 V	6.7 V	7 V	8.3 V
CL 125	Daytime	Max 1,300 rpm	——	Min 1.7 A	Max 3.0 A
	Nighttime	Max 2,000 rpm	——	Min 1.7 A	Max 3.5 A
	Battery voltage	6.3 V	——	7 V	8.3 V
CD 175	Daytime	Max 1,300 rpm	Min 3.0 A	Min 4.0 A	Max 6.0 A
	Nighttime	Max 1,800 rpm	Min 1.2 A	Min 2.0 A	Max 4.0 A
	Battery voltage	6.3 V	7 V	7 V	8.3 V
SS 125	Daytime	Max 1,300 rpm	Min 2.0 A	Min 2.5 A	Max 4.5 A
	Nighttime	Max 2,100 rpm	Min 1.2 A	Min 1.5 A	Max 4.0 A
	Battery voltage	6.4 V	6.7 V	7.5 V	8.3 V

ning, it is quite possible that the rectifier is not functioning properly (assuming that the battery is in good condition and capable of taking a charge). Before removing and testing the rectifier, make sure that it is solidly mounted on the frame. The rectifier is grounded through its mounting and will not operate without a good ground.

CAUTION: *Do not loosen or tighten the nut that holds the rectifier unit together; this will adversely affect operation of the rectifier.*

To test the rectifier, first pull apart the plastic connector, unscrew the mounting nut, and remove the rectifier unit. Inside the rectifier are four diodes which, if functioning properly, will allow electricity to pass in only one direction. To check the diodes you can use either a multimeter or a test light and the motorcyle battery. If the test light and battery are to be used, simply run a length of wire off one battery terminal and connect one of the test light leads to the other terminal. The two free wire ends will be used to check electrical continuity of the diodes.

Selenium rectifier unit.

Connect the positive lead to the yellow wire and the negative lead to the red/white wire, as shown in test one of the accompanying table. Then, reverse the leads, so that the negative lead is connected to the yellow wire and the positive lead is connected to the red/white wire. The test light should light (or the gauge needle respond) in one direction only. Repeat in the same manner for test steps two, three, and four in the table. Continuity in both directions (when reversing the leads) indicates a defective diode, in which case the rectifier unit must be replaced.

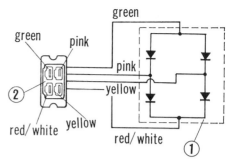

Rectifier wiring diagram. Rectifier pack (1) and connector (2).

Rectifier Test Table

Test Leads	Connection Rectifier Terminal	Resistance Value
1. $+\left(\begin{array}{c}-\\-\end{array}+\right)$	Yellow Red/white	
2. $+\left(\begin{array}{c}-\\-\end{array}+\right)$	Pink Red/white	Satisfactory if between 5 ~ 40Ω
3. $+\left(\begin{array}{c}-\\-\end{array}+\right)$	Green Yellow	
4. $+\left(\begin{array}{c}-\\-\end{array}+\right)$	Green Pink	

The diodes are quite susceptible to failure from excessive heat and electrical overload. Observe the following precautions to avoid rectifier failure.

1. Do not reverse battery polarity when installing or reconnecting the battery. The electrical system is negative ground.

2. Do not use high-voltage test equipment to test the rectifier diodes.

3. Do not run the engine with the rectifier disconnected.

4. Do not charge the battery without first disconnecting one of the battery cables.

ALTERNATOR SERVICE

Uncouple the alternator leads at the connector block and check continuity between the three stator coil leads (yellow, pink, and white) using a multimeter or a test light and battery. Connect one of the test leads to the pink wire and the other to first the yellow and then the white wire. If there is continuity in both cases, the stator coil is satisfactory. Standard stator coil resistance is 1.1 ohms (pink-to-yellow wire) and 0.55 ohm (pink-to-white wire). The stator coil assembly can be taken off after the left side cover is removed.

Starting System—All Models

The starting system consists of the starter motor and clutch, the solenoid, and the handlebar-mounted starter switch. When the button is pressed, the electrical circuit to the solenoid is closed and the solenoid is activated, sending the battery current directly to the starter motor. The starting system is quite reliable and it is unlikely that you will experience any major problems.

TESTING

If the starter will not operate, switch on the headlight and observe its intensity. If it is dim when the starter is not being operated, check the battery connections and recharge the battery. If the headlight doesn't light, check the fuse, the battery connections, the ignition switch and its connections, and check the electrical continuity of the wire between the ignition switch and the battery.

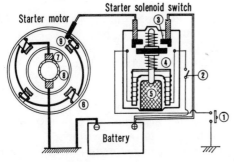

Starting system diagram.

1. Starter button switch	6. Pole
2. Ignition switch	7. Brush
3. Contact unit	8. Armature
4. Coil	9. Field coil
5. Plunger	

If the headlight is bright, press the starter button momentarily and watch the light. If it remains bright, touch a screwdriver blade between the two starter solenoid terminals. If the starter operates, connect a test light between the small yellow/red wire on the solenoid and ground. If the test light comes on as the button is pushed, the solenoid is faulty. If it does not light, look for defective wiring between the starter button and solenoid or between the starter button and ignition

switch, or simply a burned-out starter button switch. If the starter does not operate and the headlight dims as the main solenoid terminals are bridged, the starter motor is faulty. If the headlight does not dim, look for a bad connection at the starter.

If the starter motor operates freely but will not turn the engine over, the starter clutch is not operating (a rare occurrence). To remove the clutch it will be necessary to first take off the left-side crankcase cover and remove the alternator rotor.

STARTER MOTOR SERVICE

Removal and Installation

125 AND 175

1. Disconnect the electrical cable from the starter motor.
2. Take out the screws and remove the starter motor side cover.
3. Remove the left-side crankcase cover.
4. Remove the starter chain and starter motor sprocket.
5. Unscrew the three bolts and remove the starter motor.
6. Installation is a reversal of the removal procedures.

350

1. Remove the left-side rear crankcase cover and disconnect the neutral indicator switch lead.
2. Remove the left crankcase cover.
3. Remove the alternator rotor using Honda service tool no. 07011-21601 (which is a long threaded bolt that is screwed into the center of the rotor).
4. Remove the starter clutch sprocket set plate and then remove the starter motor sprocket and clutch sprocket together.
5. Disconnect the electrical cable from the starter.
6. Unscrew the two starter mounting bolts and remove the starter. The brushes can be withdrawn from their holders after the brush lead screws have been taken out.
7. Install the starter in the reverse order of removal.

450

1. Disconnect the electrical cable from the starter motor.
2. Take out the two screws and remove the starter side cover.

Starter Specification Tables

125

Item	Specification
Rated voltage	6
Rated output	0.35 kw
Intermittent operation	30 seconds
Reduction ratio	6.44

	Without Load	With Load	Lock
Voltage	5.5	4.2	2.8
Current	Max 40	120	Max 300
Torque	——	Min 0.55 kg/m	Min 1.5 kg/m
Rpm	Min 1,900–2,700	Min 400	——
Output	——	0.22 kw	——

175

Item	Specification
Rated voltage	12
Rated output	0.35 kw
Intermittent operation	30 seconds
Reduction ratio	6.44

	Without Load	With Load	Lock
Voltage	11.5	9.4	6.7
Current	Max 28	100	Max 240
Torque	——	Min 0.55 kg/m	Min 1.5 kg/m
Rpm	Min 2,000	Min 500	——
Output	——	Min 0.33 kw	——

350

Item	Specification
Rated voltage	12
Rated output	0.45 kw
Intermittent operation	30 seconds
Reduction ratio	6.44

	Without Load	With Load	Lock
Voltage	11	9	5
Current	Max 35	120	280
Torque	——	5.06 ft lbs	13.02 ft lbs
Rpm	Min 1,700	Min 500	——
Output	——	N.A.	——

450

Item	Specification
Rated voltage	12
Rated output	0.5 kw
Intermittent operation	30 seconds
Reduction ratio	6.44

	Without Load	With Load	Lock
Voltage	11	9	5
Current	Max 35	120	280
Torque	——	5.06 ft lbs	13.02 ft lbs
Rpm	Min 1,700	Min 500	——
Output	——	N.A.	——

3. Remove the left-side crankcase cover.

4. Remove the starter chain and starter motor sprocket.

5. Unscrew the three starter mounting bolts and remove the starter.

6. Install the starter in reverse order of removal.

Repair—All Models

1. Check electrical continuity between the commutator and armature core using a multimeter or test light and battery. If continuity exists, the armature coil is grounded and the armature or complete starter motor should be replaced.

2. Check continuity between the brush wired to the stator (field) coil and the starter motor cable terminal. Lack of continuity indicates an open circuit in the stator coil and the starter motor unit should be replaced.

3. Examine the carbon brushes for damage to the contact surfaces and measure their length. Replace brushes as a set if they are damaged in any way or if they measure less than 0.3 in. (7.5 mm).

4. Brush spring tension should be determined with a small pull-scale. Replace the springs if they exert less than 0.8 lb (0.4 kg) tension.

5. Polish the commutator with fine emery cloth before installing the starter motor. Check the following components for excessive wear and damage: clutch spring and rollers, bearings, bushings, the oil seal, reduction gears, and sprockets. Replace parts as necessary.

NOTE: *When reassembling the starter clutch, apply a thin coat of silicone grease to the rollers.*

STARTER SOLENOID SERVICE

The solenoid is an electromagnetic switch that closes and completes the circuit between the starter and battery when activated by the starter button. The solenoid is a necessary addition to the starting circuit because the starter button switch is not capable of handling the amperage load required to operate the starter and because mounting a heavy-duty switch on the handlebar, with the large cable needed to handle the load, is impractical.

If the solenoid does not work, check the continuity of the primary coil by connecting a multimeter or test light and battery to the two small solenoid leads. Lack of continuity indicates an open circuit and the solenoid must be replaced. If the primary coil winding is continuous, disassemble the solenoid and clean the contact points with emery paper or a small file. The points, after long use, have a tendency to become pitted or burned due to the large current passing across them.

NOTE: *Be sure to disconnect the battery before disconnecting the cables from the solenoid when it is to be removed.*

Replace the solenoid if cleaning the points fails to repair it.

Battery

Maintenance, testing, and recharging procedures for the battery are covered in chapter two.

Ignition System

The servicing and adjustment of ignition system components is covered in chapter three.

Wiring Diagrams

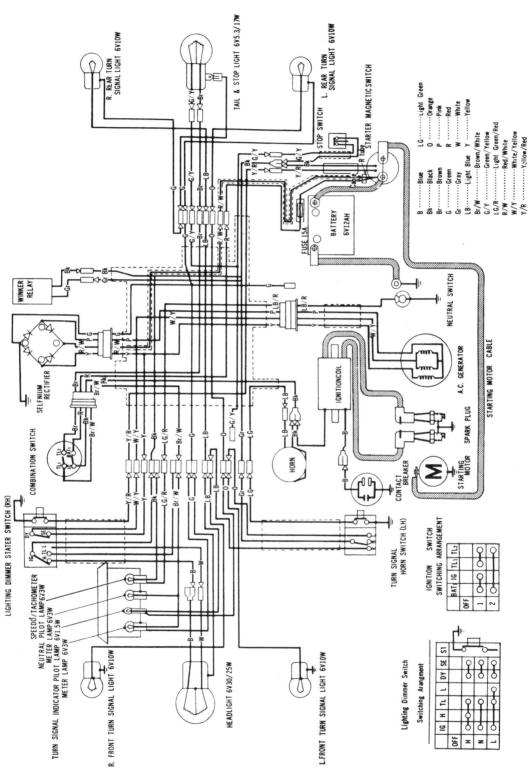

CB 125.

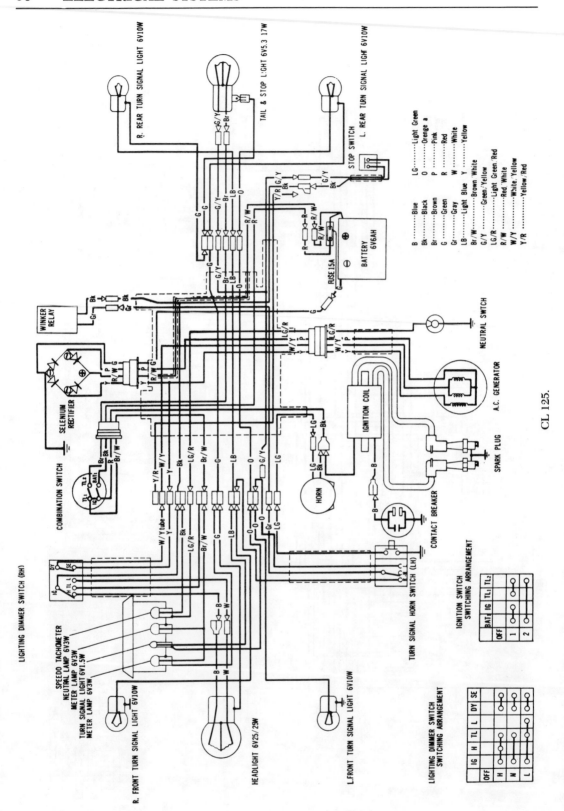

CL 125.

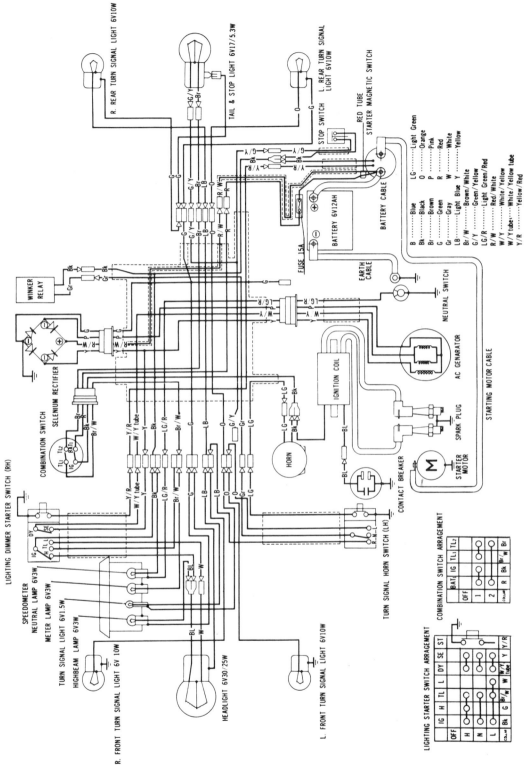

SS 125

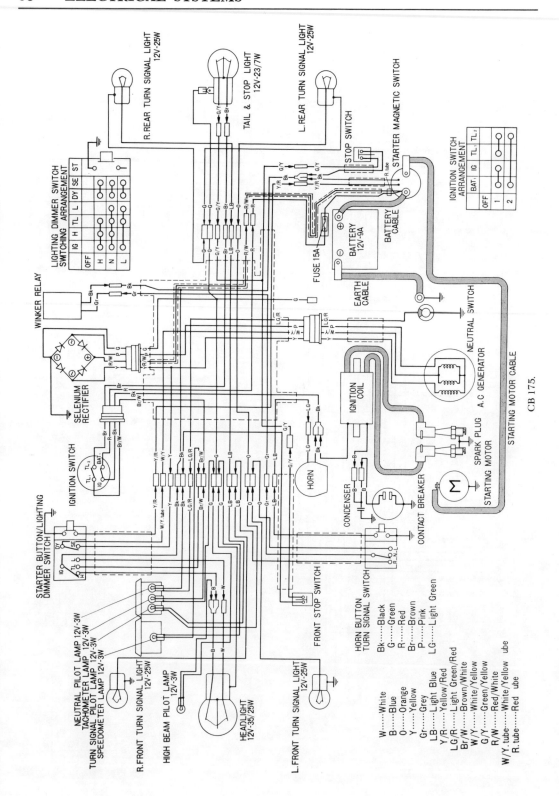

CB 175.

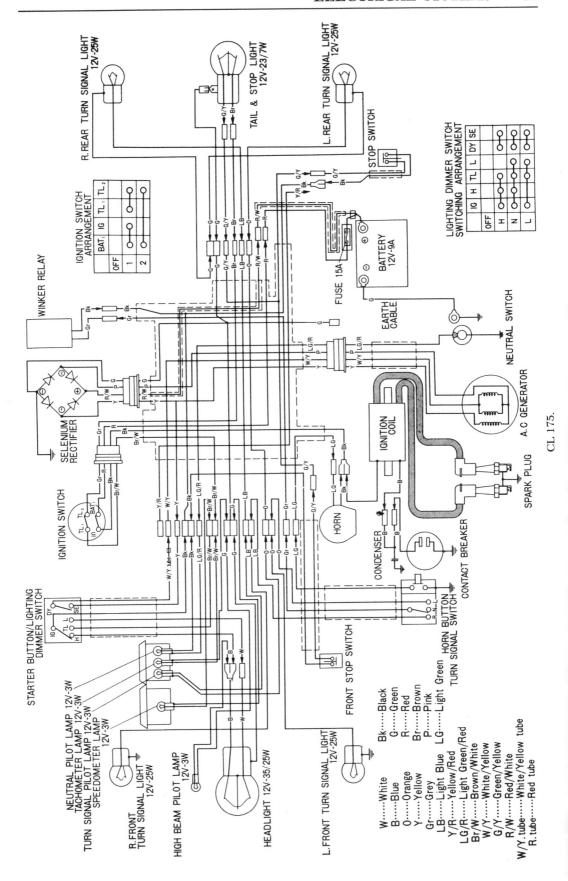

CL 175.

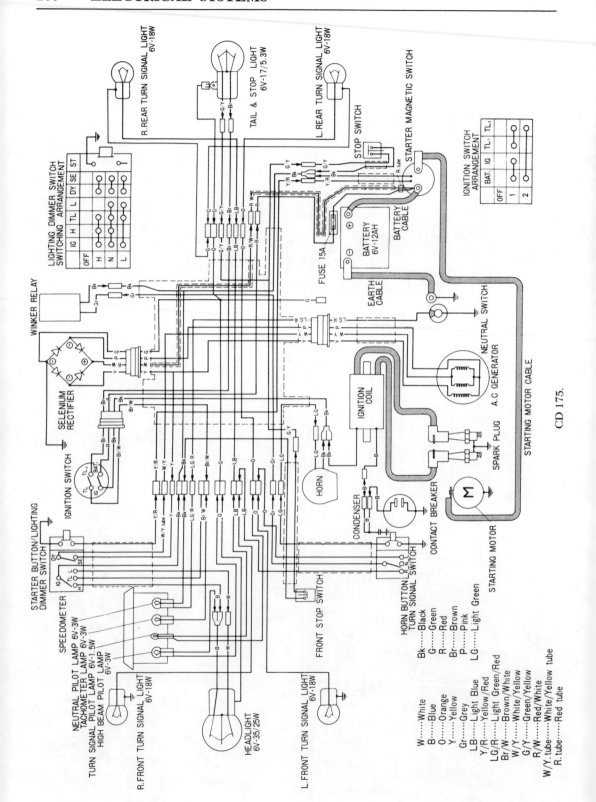

CD 175.

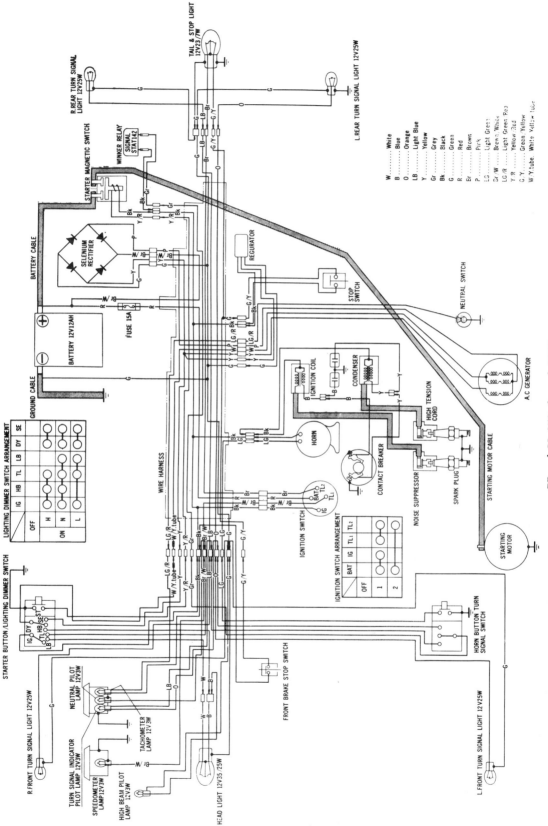

CB and CL 350, through 1969.

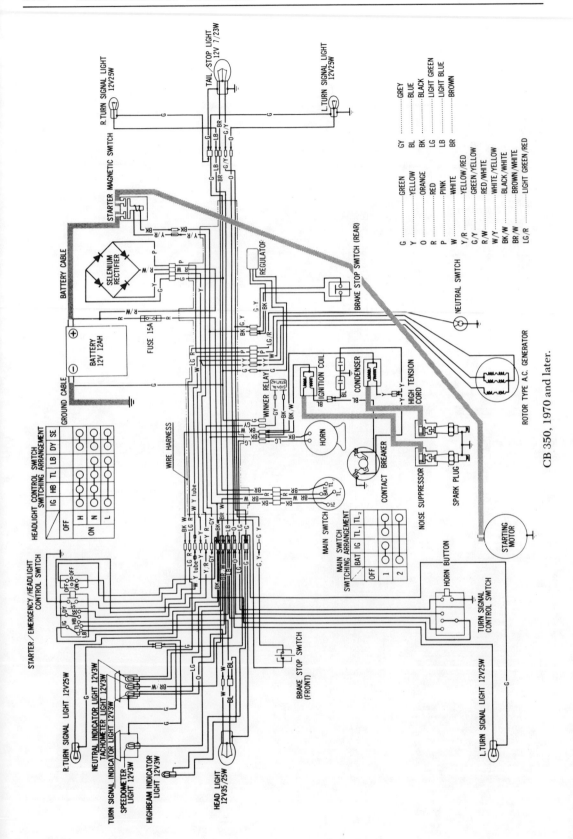

CB 350, 1970 and later.

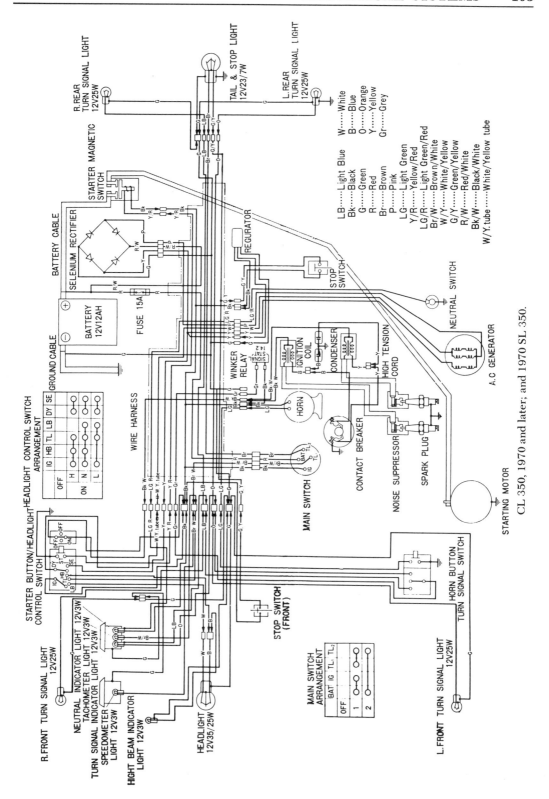

CL 350, 1970 and later; and 1970 SL 350.

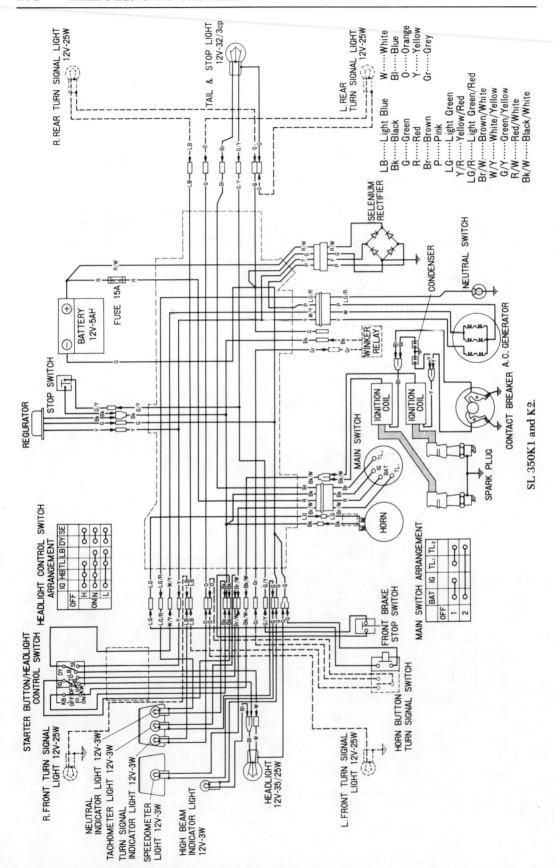

SL 350K1 and K2.

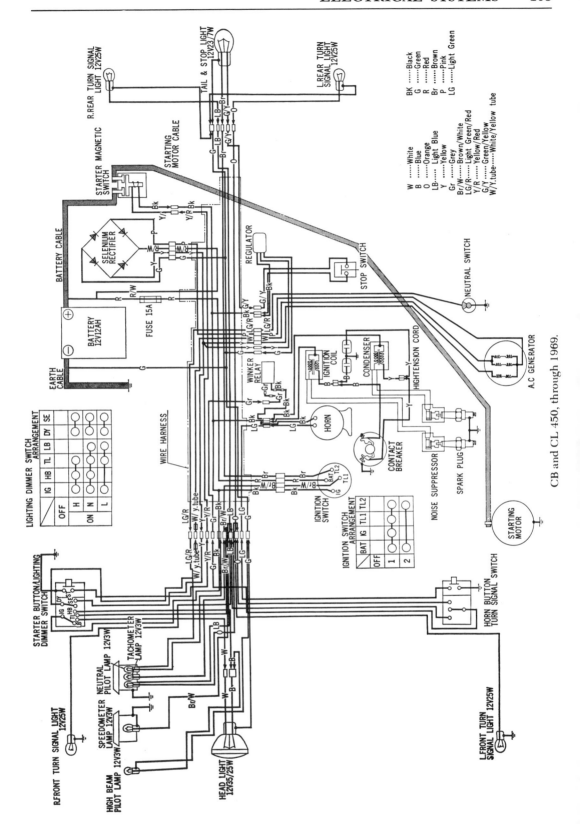

CB and CL 450, through 1969.

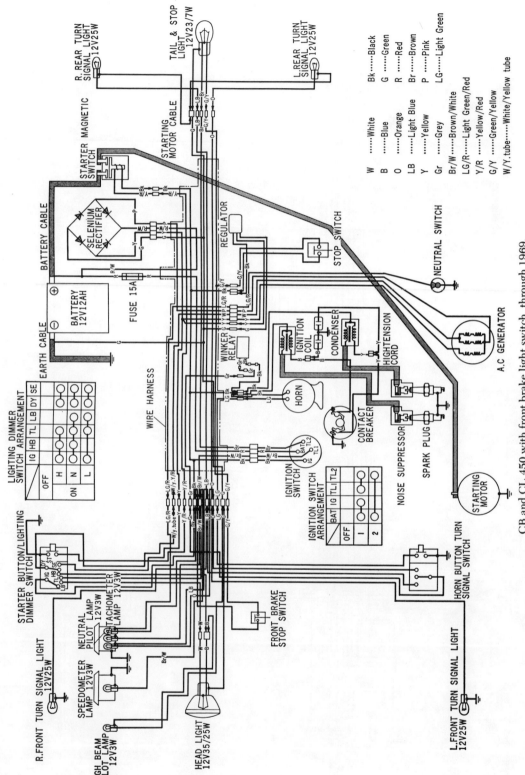

CB and CL 450 with front brake light switch, through 1969.

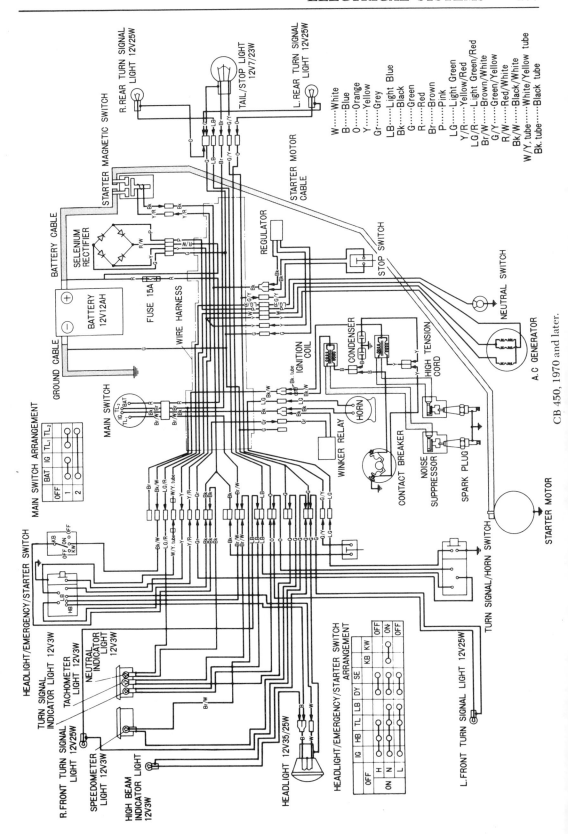

CB 450, 1970 and later.

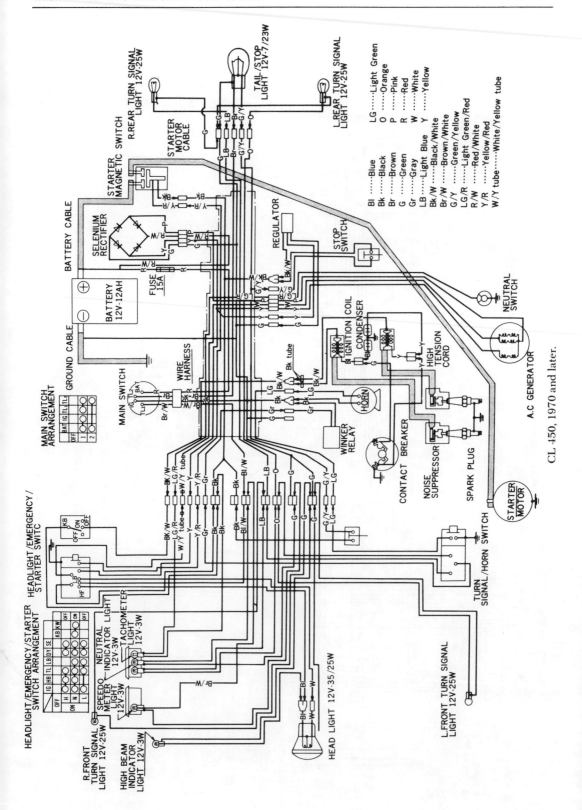

CL-450, 1970 and later.

8 · Chassis

This chapter deals with the frame, wheels, hubs, forks, etc. An important point to remember when working on these components is that they are all subject to a great deal of vibration and road shock. For this reason you should make absolutely certain that all attaching nuts and bolts are tightened securely.

Once again, cleanliness cannot be overstressed. Work in an uncluttered area with plenty of room to lay out removed parts and wash the machine thoroughly before beginning any major repairs.

Wheels and Tires

FRONT WHEEL REMOVAL AND INSTALLATION

125 and 175

1. Raise the front wheel off the ground by placing a support under the engine.
2. Disconnect the speedometer cable from the front hub.
3. Disconnect the brake cable and brake torque arm from the brake panel.
4. Unscrew the front axle nut and withdraw the axle. The wheel will drop down as the axle is pulled out.

Installation is a reversal of the removal procedure. Don't forget to readjust the brake after assembly.

350 and 450

1. Raise the front wheel off the ground by placing a support under the engine.
2. Disconnect the speedometer cable from the front hub.
3. Disconnect the brake cable and the brake torque arm (all except CB 450K4 and K5).
4. Remove the four axle clamp nuts (two on each side) and withdraw the front wheel assembly from the forks.

CAUTION: *On CB 450K4 and K5 models (disc brake), do not operate the front brake while the wheel is removed or the caliper piston will be forced out of the cylinder.*

Installation is in reverse order of removal. The front axle holder clamps are machined so that the forward mating surface is slightly higher than the rear surface, and they must be installed correctly. Place a straightedge on the mating surfaces to determine which end is higher and install the high mating surface forward. Tighten the forward retaining nut first, drawing the forward mating surface of the holder clamp flush against the fork leg mating surface, and then tighten the rear nut.

WHEEL SERVICE—ALL MODELS

Check wheel run-out at the rim using a dial indicator. If runout exceeds 0.080 in. (2.0 mm), or if the rim or spokes are dam-

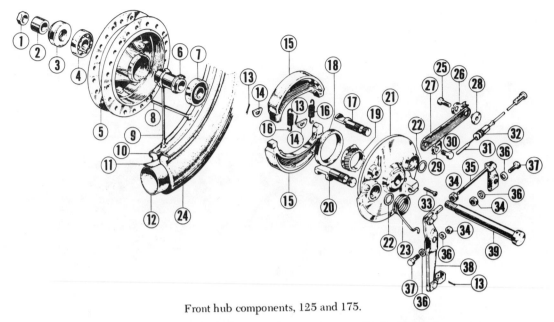

Front hub components, 125 and 175.

1. Axle nut
2. Front wheel side collar
3. Oil seal
4. Ball bearing
5. Front wheel nub
6. Front axle distance collar
7. Ball bearing
8. Spoke
9. Spoke
10. Front wheel rim
11. Tire flap
12. Front wheel tube
13. Cotter pin
14. Anchor pin washer
15. Front brake shoe
16. Front brake spring
17. Front brake cam
18. Oil seal
19. Speedometer gear
20. Front brake cam
21. Front brake panel
22. Front brake cam dust seal
23. Front brake arm return spring
24. Front wheel tire
25. Bolt
26. Tongued washer
27. Front brake stopper arm
28. Front brake stopper arm collar
29. Tongued washer
30. Front brake stopper arm bolt
31. Speedometer inner cable
32. Speedometer cable
33. 5 x 20 cross screw
34. 6 mm hex nut
35. Front brake arm B
36. 6 mm flat washer
37. 6 x 32 hex bolt
38. Front brake arm
39. Front wheel axle

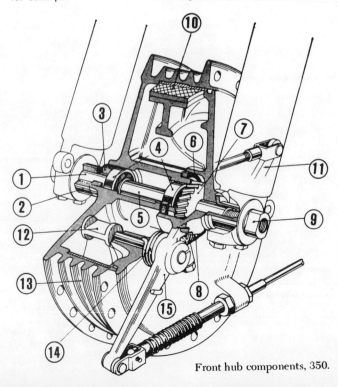

1. Front wheel axle
2. Front wheel side collar
3. Oil seal
4. Ball bearing
5. Front axle spacer
6. Oil seal
7. Speedometer gear
8. Speedometer pinion
9. Front wheel axle sleeve
10. Front brake shoe
11. Front brake cam B
12. Front brake cam
13. Front wheel hub
14. Brake arm spring
15. Front brake arm

Front hub components, 350.

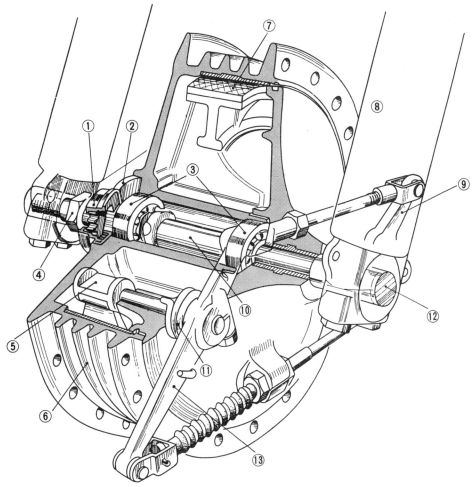

Front hub components, 450.

1. Speedometer gear box	6. Front wheel hub	11. Brake arm spring
2. Front wheel bearing retainer	7. Front brake shoe	12. Front wheel axle
3. Ball bearing	8. Brake rod	13. Front brake arm
4. Front wheel axle nut	9. Front brake arm B	
5. Front brake cam	10. Front axle spacer	

aged, the wheel should be repaired by a shop with the equipment and experience to replace and/or true the wheel properly.

FRONT WHEEL BEARING SERVICE

Disassembly

ALL MODELS EXCEPT CB 450K4 AND K5

1. Remove the front wheel.
2. Remove the front wheel axle nut and pull out the axle (350 and 450). Separate the speedometer gearbox and brake panel from the hub.
3. Remove the spacer and bearing re-

tainer (if applicable), and then remove the two wheel bearings.

CB 450K4 AND K5

1. Remove the front wheel.
2. Unscrew the axle nut and withdraw the axle and axle collar.
3. Take out the screw and remove the speedometer gearbox from the hub.
4. Bend back the locktabs, and unbolt and remove the brake disc.
5. Remove the speedometer gearbox drive flange retainer (and O-ring, K5 models only). Remove the drive flange.
6. Unscrew the wheel bearing retainer from the other side of the hub. Withdraw the bearings and spacer.

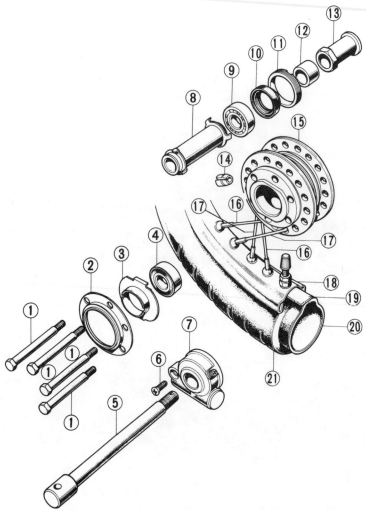

Front hub components, CB 450K4 and K5.

1. Bolt	8. Front axle spacer	15. Front wheel hub
2. Gearbox retainer cover	9. Ball bearing	16. Front spoke A
3. Gearbox retainer	10. Dust seal	17. Front spoke B
4. Ball bearing	11. Front wheel bearing retainer	18. Front wheel rim
5. Front wheel axle	12. Front wheel collar	19. Front tire flap
6. Screw	13. Front wheel axle nut	20. Front wheel tube
7. Speedometer gear box	14. Wheel balance weight	21. Front wheel tire

Inspection—All Models

Pass the axle through each bearing, in turn, and check axial and radial clearance of the bearing with a dial indicator. If axial clearance exceeds 0.004 in. (0.1 mm), or if radial clearance exceeds 0.002 in. (0.05 mm), the bearing should be replaced.

Check the bearings for smoothness of operation and for pitting of the bearing surfaces. Replace as necessary.

CAUTION: *Do not spin a dry (unlubricated) bearing at high speed.*

Assembly—All Models

Assemble in reverse order of disassembly. The following points should be noted:

ALL EXCEPT CB 450K4 AND K5

1. Pack the bearings with grease before installation.

2. The bearings incorporate a seal on the outside. Take care to install the bearings with the seal facing out.

3. Don't forget to insert the spacer before the second bearing is driven into place.

4. Install the bearings squarely in the hub. A suitably sized wrench socket or length of pipe can be used to install them.

5. Use a new oil seal and lubricate it with oil to make installation easier (except 450).

6. To avoid excessive strain on the cable, install the speedometer gearbox so that the cable is in line with the brake cable.

CB 450K4 AND K5

1. Pack the bearings with grease. Do not forget to install the spacer in the hub before installing the bearings.

2. The bearings may be driven into place using Honda service tool no. 07048-30001 or a suitably sized wrench socket or length of pipe.

3. Use a new oil seal and lubricate it with oil to make installation easier.

4. Do not forget to replace the O-ring behind the speedometer drive flange on K5 models.

FRONT WHEEL BALANCING

1. Raise the wheel off the ground and rotate it lightly. If the wheel does not rotate freely, back off the brake adjuster (turn the caliper adjuster bolt clockwise, CB 450K4 and K5) until it does.

2. Let the wheel spin until it stops on its own. The heaviest section of the wheel will stop at the lowest point.

3. Attach a weight (available in 5 g, 10 g, 15 g, and 20 g) to the spoke nipple at the highest position where the wheel has stopped. Spin the wheel again and observe where it stops. The idea is to get the proper weight positioned on the wheel so that it does not end up at any particular position when it stops spinning. Different weights may have to be tried at various positions to achieve this. Lock the weight with pliers after you've found the spot.

NOTE: *Solder may be used if weights are not available. Wrap the solder wire around the spoke nipple and secure it with tape.*

REAR WHEEL

Removal

ALL MODELS WITH REMOVABLE DRIVE CHAIN MASTER LINK

1. Place the bike on the center stand and remove the drive chain master link.

2. Unscrew the brake adjuster nut and separate the brake rod from the brake arm.

3. Unscrew the brake torque arm bolt and remove the arm from the brake panel.

4. Remove the cotter pin, unscrew the axle nut, and pull out the axle.

NOTE: *Unless you can compress the suspension enough for the axle to clear, it will be necessary to remove the muffler.*

5. Tilt the wheel slightly and remove it from the swing arm.

ALL MODELS WITH ENDLESS DRIVE CHAIN

1. Place the bike on the center stand. Unscrew the brake adjuster nut and separate the brake rod from the brake arm.

2. Unscrew the bolt and disconnect the brake torque arm from the brake panel.

3. Loosen the chain adjuster bolt on both sides. Remove the cotter pin and loosen the axle nut.

4. Remove the lockbolts and chain adjuster stop plates. Push the wheel forward and lift the chain off the rear sprocket. Withdraw the wheel rearward from the swing arm.

Installation

Install the wheel in reverse order of removal. Adjust the drive chain, if necessary, and adjust the brake. Use a new cotter pin to lock the axle nut in position.

Service

Refer to the preceding section on the front wheel.

REAR WHEEL BEARING SERVICE— ALL MODELS

Disassembly

1. Remove the wheel and withdraw the axle from the hub.

2. Take out the circlip, bend back the locktabs, and unbolt the rear sprocket.

3. Remove the oil seal internal retainer (125 and 175). Unscrew the bearing retainer (350 and 450).

4. Remove the bearings and spacer for the hub.

Inspection

Pass the axle through each bearing, in turn, and measure the axial and diametrical clearance of the bearing with a dial in-

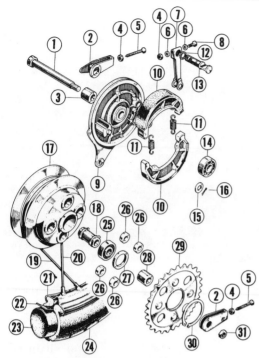

Rear hub components, 125 and 175.

1. Rear wheel axle
2. Drive chain adjuster
3. Rear brake panel side collar
4. Nut
5. Drive chain adjusting bolt
6. 6 mm flat washer
7. Rear brake arm
8. Bolt
9. Rear brake panel
10. Rear brake shoe
11. Brake shoe spring
12. Brake cam dust seal
13. Rear brake cam
14. Ball bearing
15. Handle holder setting washer A
16. Cotter pin
17. Rear wheel hub
18. Rear axle spacer
19. Spoke
20. Spoke
21. Rear wheel rim
22. Tire flap
23. Rear wheel tube
24. Rear tire
25. Ball bearing
26. Rear wheel damper bushing
27. Oil seal
28. Rear wheel side collar
29. Final driven sprocket
30. Circlip
31. Axle nut

dicator. If axial clearance exceeds 0.004 in. (0.1 mm), or if diametrical clearance exceeds 0.0024 in. (0.06 mm), the bearing should be replaced.

Check the bearings for smoothness of operation and for pitting of the bearing surfaces. Replace as necessary.

Check to see if the axle is bent by rolling it on a flat surface. A bent axle should be replaced.

Assembly

Assemble in reverse order of disassembly. Note the following points:

1. Pack the bearings with grease. Do not forget to install the spacer in the hub before installing the second bearing.

2. The bearings may be driven into place using a suitably sized wrench socket or length of pipe.

3. Use a new oil seal and lubricate it with oil to make installation into the bearing retainer easier.

4. Use thread-lock cement on the bearing retainer (350 and 450).

5. Apply a small quantity of grease to the friction surfaces of the flange and wheel hub.

REAR WHEEL BALANCING

Refer to the section on front wheel balancing. Procedures are the same, except that if the rear wheel is to be balanced while mounted on the bike, the chain must be removed from the rear sprocket so the wheel will spin freely. Back off the brake adjuster nut if necessary to allow the wheel to spin.

TIRE REMOVAL AND INSTALLATION, FRONT AND REAR

1. Remove the wheel.

2. Lay the wheel on a cloth or piece of cardboard to protect the hub.

3. Remove the valve core and the valve stem retaining nut.

4. Step down on the tire to break it loose from the rim (on both sides).

5. Use two small tire irons, placed near the valve stem about 5 in. apart, to pry the tire bead over the rim while depressing the bead opposite the irons. Remove one iron and work around the rim until the bead is clear of the rim all the way around.

CAUTION: *Be very careful not to pinch the tube with the tire irons.*

6. Remove the tube and, if the tire is to be replaced, lever the other bead over the rim in the same manner. If the tube has been removed to repair a puncture, be

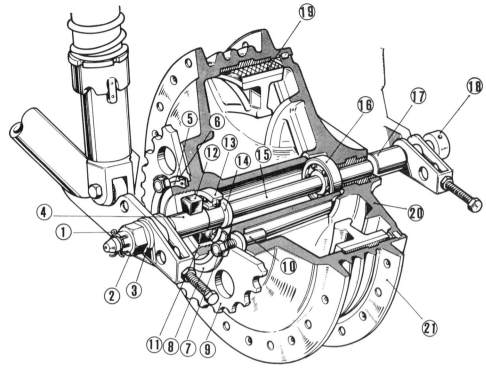

Rear hub components, 350.

1. Cotter pin	8. 10 mm tongued washer	15. Rear axle spacer
2. 10 mm castle nut	9. Final driven sprocket	16. Ball bearing
3. Washer	10. Driven sprocket fixing bolt	17. Rear wheel collar
4. Rear wheel side collar	11. Rear wheel bearing retainer	18. Rear wheel axle
5. External circlip	12. Dust seal	19. Rear brake shoe
6. 70 mm washer	13. Ball bearing	20. Rear wheel brake panel
7. 10 mm thin nut	14. Rear axle spacer	21. Rear wheel hub

sure to check the tire casing for the cause of the flat and for damage.

Installation is accomplished in the following manner:

1. Coat the tire beads with tire mounting solution or liquid detergent. If the tire has been removed from the rim, lever one side onto the rim.

2. Install the valve core in the stem, inflate the tube *slightly*, and install it into the tire casing. Insert the valve stem into the valve stem hole in the rim. Partially install the valve stem retaining nut to hold the tube in position.

3. It will now be possible to slip about ¾ of the bead over the rim by hand. The remaining section can be positioned using a rubber mallet or the tire irons. Again, if the irons are used, be careful not to pinch the tube.

4. Rotate the tire on the rim until the balance mark on the tire aligns with the valve stem.

5. Inflate the tire to about 40 psi and then deflate it completely. This will ensure that the beads are seated properly and that the tube will not be deformed when reinflated. Inflate to the correct pressure and tighten the valve stem retaining nut.

Brakes

DESCRIPTION

Except for the SL 175 and late-model CB 450s, all twin-cylinder Hondas use a double leading shoe brake at the front wheel. (The SL 175 has a single leading shoe brake at the front.) All models incorporate a single leading shoe brake at the rear. A double leading shoe brake differs from the single leading shoe type in that both ends of the brake shoes are forced

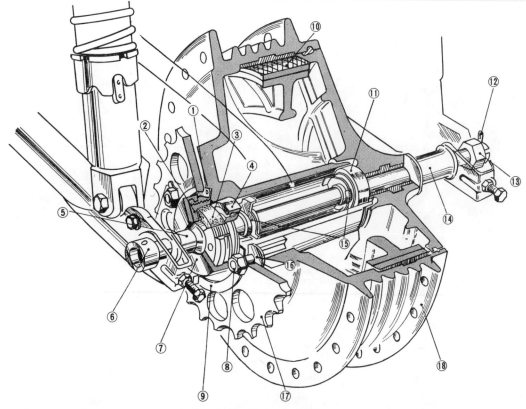

Rear hub components, 450.

1. 73.8 mm circlip	7. Bearing retainer	13. Rear axle nut
2. Rear wheel bearing retainer	8. 10 mm nut	14. Rear brake panel collar
3. Dust seal	9. 10 mm tongue washer	15. Rear axle spacing collar
4. Ball bearing	10. Rear brake shoe	16. Driven sprocket bolt
5. Rear wheel side collar	11. Ball bearing	17. Final driven sprocket
6. Rear wheel axle	12. 4.0 x 10 mm center pin	18. Rear wheel hub

against the brake drum as the brakes are applied, rather than having one end of each shoe forced out while the other end merely rests on a pivot. The advantage of a double leading shoe brake is that it provides greater braking power with less effort required than a comparable single leading shoe brake. Its disadvantages are that it is sometimes difficult to modulate its power smoothly, producing grabbiness, and that a double leading shoe brake has very little reverse braking power, so that it is hard to hold the bike from rolling backwards while standing on a hill. Thus, the self-energizing characteristics of the double leading shoe brake which are responsible for its power are also responsible for its weaknesses.

The hydraulic disc brake used on the CB 450K4 and K5 is quite simple in design and offers no special service problems. The components incorporated into the disc brake system include the brake fluid reservoir and master cylinder, mounted on the handlebar. Operating the brake lever actuates the master cylinder which draws fluid from the reservoir and transfers it under pressure through the hydraulic lines to the caliper assembly, mounted on the left fork leg. The caliper assembly consists of the caliper body, caliper piston, and two friction pads. It is of the single-piston floating type with the piston acting directly only on the pad adjacent to it, when responding to pressure from the master cylinder. The caliper mounting allows it to move slightly along the front axle centerline, and the reaction force generated when the pad adjacent to the piston contacts the brake disc is used to move the caliper assembly over, thus pulling the opposite pad into contact with the disc. The brake disc, bolted to the front wheel hub, efficiently absorbs and dissipates the heat resulting from frictional contact with the pads. A hydraulically operated brake light switch is located at the hydraulic line junction near the headlight. The advantages of the disc brake are that it is, generally, more powerful than a drum brake of similar weight, has a greater resistance to fade and a more progressive action, enabling greater control and shorter stopping distances, and it is less affected by water.

FRONT BRAKE SERVICE

Drum Brake

SHOE REPLACEMENT

The brake shoes should be replaced when the brake cable and operating lever at the brake panel move over-center or past perpendicular as the brake is applied. The replacement procedure is as follows:

1. Remove the wheel.
2. Remove the axle and separate the brake panel from the brake drum.
3. On the 125 and 175 models, the brake shoes can be removed after the two cotter pins and the anchor pin washer have been taken off. On the 350 and 450, first remove the brake levers from the panel and then spread the shoes apart and lift them away.

Front brake panel assembly (175 shown). Brake shoes (1), cotter pins (2), and anchor pin washers (3).

4. Minimum acceptable lining thickness is 0.080 in. (2.0 mm). Shoes must always be replaced as a set.
5. Examine the brake actuating cams for wear and replace them if they are damaged. Apply a *light* coat of grease to the cams, and then install the shoes and springs as removed. If the brake shoe

springs are stretched or damaged, they should be replaced.
6. Wipe the brake drum clean and examine it for damage and wear. Light scoring can be tolerated, but the drum should be replaced if badly scored or worn out of round.
7. Assemble the drum and hub, and reinstall the wheel.
8. Adjust the brake operating lever interconnecting rod on double leading shoe brakes so that both ends of the shoes contact the drum at the same time. Finally, adjust the cable so that there is about ½ in. of free-play at the handlebar lever.

Disc Brake

PAD REPLACEMENT

To determine pad wear on the CB 450K4, measure the clearance between the front of the caliper and the disc face using a feeler gauge. When clearance is less than 0.08 in. (2.0 mm), the pads should be replaced.

Pads should be replaced on the K5 (1972) model when either one has worn down to the red wear indicator groove.

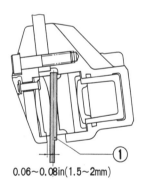

0.06~0.08in(1.5~2mm)

Replace disc pads on the 450K4 when clearance between the disc (1) and caliper is less than 0.08 in.

1. Remove the front wheel.
2. Using the proper size allen wrench, remove the two bolts from the side of the caliper and remove the right-side caliper half.
3. Remove the pad from the piston side of the caliper. Withdraw the cotter pin and remove the pad from the other caliper half.
4. Before installing the new pads, apply a small amount of silicone grease to the pad sliding surfaces on the caliper, as

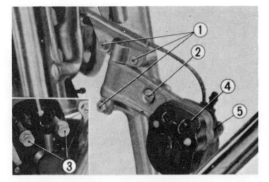

1. Caliper mounting bolts
2. Caliper adjusting bolt
3. Caliper half retaining bolts
4. Right caliper
5. Left caliper

1. Nut   4. Brake disc
2. Caliper adjusting bolt   5. Left pad
3. Right pad

shown. The grease serves to keep pad operation smooth by repelling dust and water as well as providing lubrication. Use grease sparingly and do not allow it to contact the pad friction material.

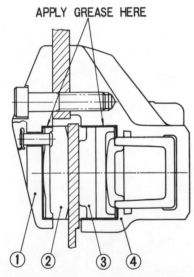

APPLY GREASE HERE

1. Right caliper half   3. Left brake pad
2. Right brake pad   4. Left caliper half

5. Install the new pads in the caliper halves and bolt the caliper together.

6. Install the front wheel and adjust the brake as explained in the following section. Avoid heavy braking until at least 500 miles have been covered.

AJUSTMENT

1. Loosen the caliper adjuster bolt locknut and turn the bolt until the inside pad (closest to the wheel) lightly contacts the disc.

About 0.006 in. clearance should exist between the pads and disc.

1. Caliper assembly   3. Nut
2. Brake pads   4. Caliper adjusting bolt

2. Turn the adjuster bolt in the opposite direction until the front wheel rotates with as little drag as possible (about 1/4–1/2 turn) and tighten the locknut.

CALIPER SERVICE

Leakage of brake fluid from around the caliper piston indicates that the caliper assembly is worn or damaged, and the cause should be investigated immediately. To remove, inspect, and rebuild the caliper assembly:

1. Remove the front wheel.

2. Unscrew the hydraulic line connection at the caliper. Catch the fluid that drains from the line in a suitable container and dispose of it. Do not reuse old brake fluid.

3. Unscrew the three caliper mounting bolts at the left fork leg and remove the caliper.

4. Remove the two bolts and separate the caliper halves.

5. Remove the pad seat from the caliper piston and withdraw the piston.

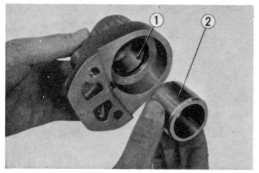

The left caliper half (1) and piston (2). The piston seal is visible in the caliper bore. 450K4 shown.

6. Remove the seal from the cylinder using a plastic or wood instrument to avoid damaging the bore.

7. Examine the cylinder bore and piston surface for scoring and pitting, and replace if damaged. Cylinder bore diameter should not exceed 1.540 in. (38.215 mm), and piston diameter should not be less than 1.500 in. (38.105 mm). Maximum calculated clearance between the piston and cylinder is 0.0045 in. (0.115 mm). Replace parts as necessary. Clean all components and dry with compressed air.

8. Use a new seal in the cylinder bore and lubricate it thoroughly with fresh brake fluid before installing. Make sure it is seated properly in its groove.

9. Lubricate the piston with brake fluid and install it in the cylinder. Be careful not to twist the seal or force it out of the groove. Install the pad seat on the piston.

10. Reinstall the brake pads in the caliper halves. Use new pads if the old ones have been in contact with brake fluid.

11. Bolt the caliper halves together and remount the caliper assembly on the fork leg.

12. Connect the hydraulic line and replace the front wheel. Bleed and adjust the brake (refer to the appropriate headings in this section).

MASTER CYLINDER SERVICE

Brake fluid leakage around the brake lever and excessive lever travel (after bleeding the brake to make sure that there is no air trapped in the hydraulic system) are indications of master cylinder malfunction. The rebuilding procedure is as follows:

NOTE: *Be very careful when filling or emptying the reservoir. Brake fluid can damage paint and plastic, and extreme care should be exercised in handling the stuff. Wipe up any spills immediately.*

1. Place a cloth underneath the connection to absorb any spilled fluid, and disconnect the brake hose from the master cylinder.

2. Unscrew the clamp bolts and remove

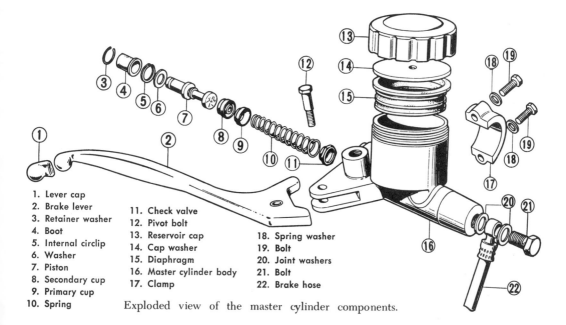

1. Lever cap
2. Brake lever
3. Retainer washer
4. Boot
5. Internal circlip
6. Washer
7. Piston
8. Secondary cup
9. Primary cup
10. Spring
11. Check valve
12. Pivot bolt
13. Reservoir cap
14. Cap washer
15. Diaphragm
16. Master cylinder body
17. Clamp
18. Spring washer
19. Bolt
20. Joint washers
21. Bolt
22. Brake hose

Exploded view of the master cylinder components.

the master cylinder from the handlebar. Unscrew the reservoir cap and discard the brake fluid.

3. Remove the rubber boot. Remove the circlip and withdraw the washer, piston, seal, spring cap, spring, and check valve.

4. Check the cylinder bore for scoring and pitting, and measure the wear using a dial indicator. Bore diameter should not exceed 0.553 in. (14.055 mm). Replace the master cylinder assembly if damaged or worn.

5. Clean all components in solvent and dry with compressed air.

6. Use a new seal and lubricate it with fresh brake fluid. Install the components in the bore as removed.

7. Mount the master cylinder on the handlebar and connect the brake hose. Do not forget to install the two washers at the connection. (Use brake fluid conforming to SAE specification J1703).

BLEEDING THE HYDRAULIC BRAKE SYSTEM

The purpose of bleeding the brake is to expel any air trapped in the hydraulic system. Air, since it is compressible, will cause the brake lever to feel spongy and will decrease braking effectiveness. If the brake lever begins to feel spongy for no apparent reason, it is likely that there is a fault in the hydraulic system. It would be wise to determine and remedy the fault rather than merely bleed the brake and hope the problem will disappear.

The brake hydraulic system must be bled whenever any part of the system has been disconnected or removed for service. When refilling the master cylinder reservoir, use only brake fluid conforming to SAE specification J1703. Any brand meeting this requirement is acceptable. The brake fluid container of all reputable brands will be plainly marked with the standards the fluid meets or exceeds.

1. Top up the reservoir with brake fluid and replace the cap to keep dirt and moisture out and the fluid in.

2. Attach one end of a small rubber hose to the bleed valve at the caliper and place the other end in a container to catch the fluid.

3. Pump the brake lever rapidly several times until some resistance is felt and, holding the lever against the resistance, open the bleed valve about ½ turn. When

the lever bottoms, close the valve (do not overtighten) and then release the lever.

4. Repeat this operation until no more air is released from the hose and the brake lever is firm in operation. Check the fluid level in the reservoir often to make sure it doesn't go dry and draw more air into the system. Do not reuse fluid that has been pumped out of the system. Do not use fluid that has been stored for more than a few weeks after the seal on its container has been opened, as brake fluid will absorb moisture from the air and may corrode the master cylinder and caliper. Be sure to refill the reservoir to the level mark (do not overfill) when through. Avoid overtightening the cap or the fluid will weep from around the cap edge.

DISC SERVICE

The brake disc normally requires no service of any kind. However, if the disc becomes scored for any reason it should be replaced and a new set of pads should be installed. A badly scored disc will reduce the effectiveness of the brake and shorten pad life considerably. If the front brake lever oscillates or fluctuates when the brake is applied at speed, the indication is that the brake disc is warped or bent. Check the run-out of the disc with a dial indicator and replace it if run-out exceeds 0.012 in. (0.3 mm). To replace the disc:

1. Remove the front wheel.

2. Bend back the locktabs, unscrew the six nuts, and remove the disc from the hub.

3. Mount the new disc on the hub and tighten the nuts evenly, using new locktabs to secure them.

4. Examine the brake pads and replace them if they are close to the limit of wear or have worn in an unusual pattern.

5. Install the wheel on the bike and check brake adjustment.

REAR BRAKE SERVICE— ALL MODELS

Brake Shoe Replacement

The brake shoes should be replaced when the brake operating rod (or cable) and lever move over-center or past perpendicular as the brake is applied. The replacement procedure is as follows:

1. Remove the rear wheel.

2. Unscrew the axle nut and withdraw

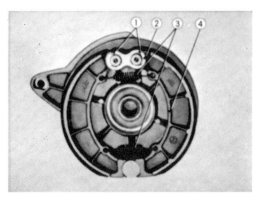

Rear brake panel assembly (450 shown). Cotter pins (1), pivot (2), springs (3), and brake shoe (4).

the axle (CB 450K4 and K5). Separate the brake panel from the hub.

3. Remove the cotter pin and washer from the brake shoe pivots and lift the shoes away from the brake panel. Minimum acceptable lining thickness at any point is 0.080 in. (2.0 mm).

4. Apply a light coat of grease to the brake shoe pivots and the actuating cam. Install the shoes and springs as removed, using new cotter pins. (Use new springs if the original ones are stretched or damaged.)

5. Wipe the brake drum clean with a cloth and examine for scoring and wear. Light scoring can be tolerated, but the drum should be replaced if badly scored or worn out of round.

6. Assemble the drum and hub, and install the wheel. Adjust the brake so that there is about 1.0 in. free-play at the pedal. Avoid heavy braking until at least 500 miles have been covered.

Final Drive

CHAIN INSPECTION

The chain should be regularly inspected for wear and damage in the following manner:

1. Place the bike on the center stand and thoroughly lubricate the chain.

2. Measure the amount of slack at the middle of the chain run and, if slack exceeds 1.5 in., adjust the chain. Refer to chapter two.

3. Turn the wheel slowly and examine the chain for:

a) damaged rollers,
b) loose pins,
c) rusted links,
d) binding or kinked links.

Replace the chain if the rollers are damaged or the pins are loose, or if rusted or binding links cannot be worked free with lubrication.

SPROCKET INSPECTION

Check the sprockets for broken or worn teeth. Worn sprocket teeth have a hooked, assymetrical appearance. If the side of the sprocket is worn, the indication is that the sprockets are misaligned. In any case of wear or damage, the sprocket should be replaced. Remember that worn sprockets can ruin a good chain, and vice versa. Do not hesitate to replace the chain and both sprockets, if need be, to avoid costly and dangerous chain failure.

CHAIN REMOVAL AND INSTALLATION

ALL MODELS EXCEPT CB 450K4 AND K5

The chain can be separated and pulled off the sprockets after the master link has been removed. Threading the chain back onto the countershaft sprocket is made easier if you have an old length of chain lying around that you can hook onto the chain on the bike as it is removed. Leave the old chain draped over the sprocket so that you can hook the good chain back onto it and pull it over the sprocket when you are ready to reinstall it. Be sure to install the master link clip with the closed end facing in the direction of forward rotation of the chain.

CB 450K AND K5

To remove the endless chain used on these models it is necessary to use a chain breaking tool. A heavy-duty chain breaker is available from Honda dealers, part number 07062-30050. To break the chain using this tool:

1. Grind or file the pins of the link to be removed flush with the link side plate. Do not cut the chain at the master link (identifiable by the depression in the pin centers).

2. Swing the pin seat backing plate on the chain breaker away from the pin seat and place one of the link rollers in the holding lugs of the tool.

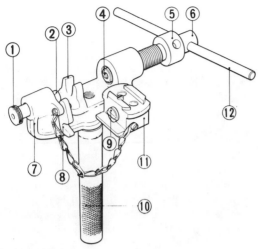

Chain breaker.

1. Pin seat knob
2. Pin seat
3. Holder
4. Cotter pin
5. Main bolt
6. Link removal bolt
7. Body
8. Pin seat backing plate
9. Wedge
10. Grip
11. Guide
12. Lever

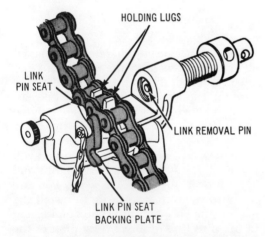

3. Seat the main bolt against the side plate of the link and turn the link removal bolt in until the pin is driven out.

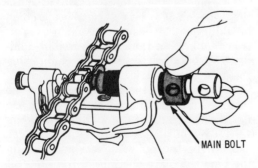

4. Place the other link roller in the holding lugs and repeat step three.

To install a new master link (replacing the chain on the motorcycle):

1. Insert the master link through the ends of the chain so that the side plate is inside (closest to the wheel).

2. Place one of the master link rollers in the holding lugs of the tool with the pins facing the main bolt.

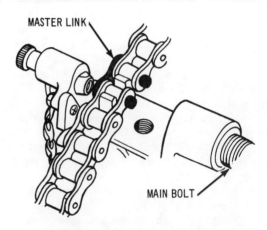

3. Push the pin seat knob in until it contacts the pin and swing the pin seat backing plate over to lock the pin seat in position.

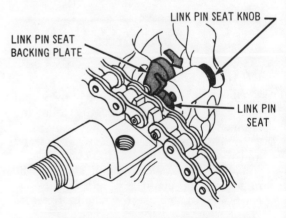

4. Place the master link side plate in the guide block, as shown, so that the stamped

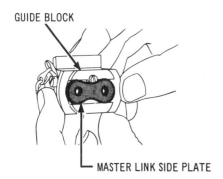

GUIDE BLOCK

MASTER LINK SIDE PLATE

letters or numbers on the plate face the surface of the guide block (facing out when installed on the chain).

5. Back out the link removal bolt until it is behind the nose of the main bolt.

CAUTION: *The link removal bolt will be damaged if it is allowed to protrude beyond the nose of the main bolt.*

6. Place the guide block in the tool with the master link side plate against the pins. Make sure that the pins are aligned with the holes in the side plate.

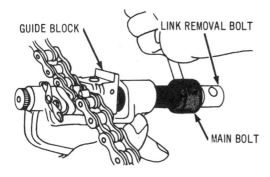

GUIDE BLOCK   LINK REMOVAL BOLT

MAIN BOLT

7. Turn the main bolt in until the pins pass through the plate and seat against the recess in the guide block.

8. Reposition the guide block so that the staking die faces the pin and the protruding shoulder of the guide block is below the side plate.

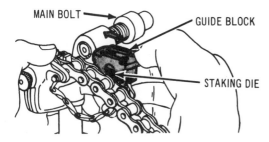

MAIN BOLT   GUIDE BLOCK

STAKING DIE

9. Turn the main bolt in until the staking die contacts the pin and check to make sure that the die is centered across the pin.

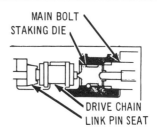

MAIN BOLT
STAKING DIE

DRIVE CHAIN
LINK PIN SEAT

10. Turn the main bolt in an additional ¾ turn to stake the pin. Repeat steps 8–10 for the other master link pin. Examine both pins to make sure they are properly staked.

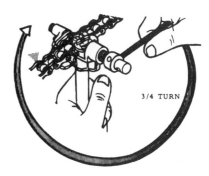

3/4 TURN

CAUTION: *The main bolt must be turned no more or no less than ¾ turn. Less than ¾ turn will not secure the side plate properly, and more than ¾ turn may crack the pin.*

SPROCKET REMOVAL AND INSTALLATION—ALL MODELS

To gain access to the countershaft sprocket it is only necessary to remove the left-side rear crankcase cover. The sprocket can be unbolted after the locktabs (if applicable) are bent back. Loosen or remove the chain and then remove the sprocket.

REAR HUB DAMPER SERVICE

1. Remove the rear wheel assembly.

2. Remove the axle assembly (CB 450K4 and K5). Bend back the locktabs and unbolt the sprocket.

3. Remove the circlip, separate the sprocket from the hub, and remove the damper rubbers. Replace damaged or worn dampers as a complete set.

4. Reassemble the hub and wheel in reverse order of disassembly. Use new locktabs to secure the sprocket nuts.

CHAIN OILER ADJUSTMENT— CB 450K4 AND K5

1. Remove the countershaft sprocket cover (left-side rear crankcase cover) and wipe the sprocket and chain clean.

2. Turn the oiler adjusting screw in until seated (fully closed).

Chain oiler adjusting screw (1).

3. Ride the bike a minute or two at about 50–60 mph and then check the oil output to the chain. If additional oiling is desired, back the adjusting screw out about 1/4 turn and recheck output. Maximum oiling is achieved when the screw is backed out three full turns from closed.

NOTE: *Since the chain is lubricated with oil from the engine crankcase, the engine oil level should be checked frequently to make sure that it does not run low.*

Front Suspension

FORK SERVICE
125 and 175—All Models
DISASSEMBLY

1. Remove the front wheel.

2. Unscrew the mounting bolts and remove the fender.

3. Partially loosen the two headlight shell mounting bolts.

4. Unscrew the two top fork bolts and loosen the two lower triple clamp pinch-bolts. Pull the fork legs out from the bottom.

5. Raise the fork dust seal (if applicable) and remove the oil seal circlip. Separate the bottom fork leg case from the fork tube and discard the oil in the bottom fork leg.

6. Carefully pry out the oil seal, taking care not to damage the inside surface of the bottom fork leg.

INSPECTION

Examine all components for damage and scoring. If the fork assembly was not operating properly, check the spring height and damper component dimensions against the specifications in the accompanying table. Clean all components in sol-

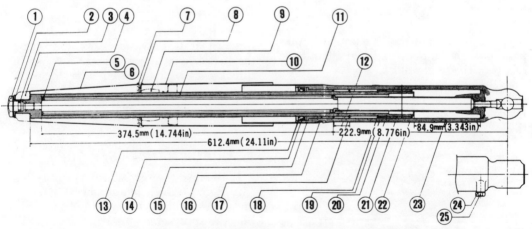

Cross-section of fork leg; CB and SS 125, CB and CD 175.

1. Front fork bolt	9. Steering stem	17. Fork pipe stopper ring
2. Front fork washer	10. Front fork under cover	18. Fork valve stopper ring
3. O-ring	11. Front fork pipe complete	19. Front damper valve
4. Fork top bridge	12. Rebound stroke (19 mm : 0.748 in.)	20. Piston stopper ring
5. Front cushion spring	13. 41 mm internal circlip	21. Front fork piston
6. Front fork upper cover	14. Front fork oil seal	22. Fork piston snap-ring
7. Front fork rib	15. Bottom case cover	23. Front fork bottom case comp.
8. Front fork rib packing	16. Front fork pipe guide	24. Fork drain cock packing
		25. Bolt

Fork Specifications (in./mm)

	CB/CL/SS 125	CB/175	CL/SL 175	CB/CL 350
Spring free-length:				
nominal	16.331/414.8	16.331/414.8	N.A.	8.27/210
minimum	15.1/384	15.1/384	N.A.	7.72/196
Damper piston:				
minimum diameter	1.395/35.42	1.395/35.42	1.394/35.4	1.472/37.39
maximum taper	0.002/0.04	0.002/0.04	0.002/0.04	N.A.
Lower fork leg case:				
maximum inside diameter	1.406/35.72	1.406/35.72	N.A.	1.484/37.68
maximum taper	0.002/0.04	0.002/0.04	0.002/0.04	N.A.

	SL 350	CB/CL 450 up to 1970	CB 450K4	CB 450K5
Spring free-length:				
nominal	N.A.	8.35/211.9	19.075/484.5	17.78/451.7
minimum	N.A.	8.06/205	18.11/460	16.73/425
Damper piston:				
minimum diameter	1.472/37.39	1.551/39.4	1.551/39.4	N.A.
maximum taper	N.A.	0.002/0.03	0.001/0.02	N.A.
Lower fork leg case:				
maximum inside diameter	1.484/37.68	N.A.	1.559/39.68	N.A.
maximum taper	N.A.	N.A.	0.0012/0.03	N.A.

vent and dry thoroughly. Even a small piece of grit can impair damper action. Make sure that the slider tube is not bent by rolling it on a flat surface. Replace if bent.

ASSEMBLY

Assemble in reverse order of disassembly. Observe the following points:

1. Lubricate the seal with oil before installation. If the proper oil seal driver is not available, a piece of wood cut to fit the inside of the bottom fork leg will do the job without damaging the inside surface.

2. New fork piston stopper rings and circlips should be used since the old parts may be fatigued and liable to break.

3. Before tightening the lower triple clamp pinch-bolts, insert the axle through the fork legs to make sure that they are level.

4. Fill the forks with the proper amount

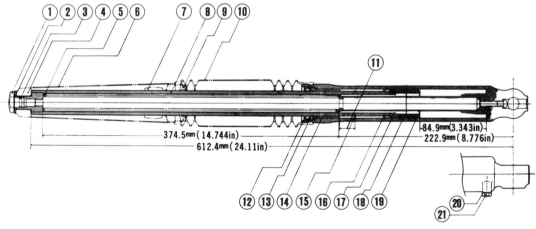

Cross-section of fork leg; CL 125.

1. Front fork bolt	8. Front fork pipe comp	15. Fork pipe stopper ring
2. Front fork washer	9. Front fork dust seal	16. Fork valve stopper ring
3. O-ring	10. Front fork boot	17. Piston stopper ring
4. Fork top bridge	11. Rebound stroke (19 mm : 0.748 in.)	18. Front fork piston
5. Front cushion spring	12. 41 mm internal circlip	19. Fork piston snap-ring
6. Front fork cover	13. Front fork oil seal	20. Fork drain cock packing
7. Steering stem	14. Front fork pipe guide	21. Bolt

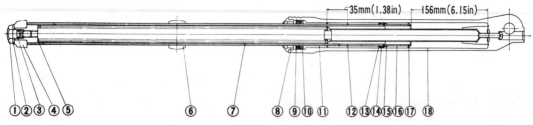

Cross-section of fork leg; CL and SL 175.

1. Front fork bolt	7. Front fork pipe	13. Fork valve stopper ring
2. 24 mm washer	8. Front fork dust seal	14. Front damper valve
3. O-ring	9. 41 mm internal circlip	15. Fork piston stopper ring
4. Front fork top bridge	10. Front fork oil seal	16. Front fork piston
5. Front cushion spring	11. Front fork pipe guide	17. Fork piston snap ring
6. Front fork bottom bridge	12. Front piston stopper ring	18. Front fork bottom case

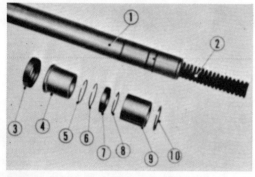

Damper components.

1. Front fork pipe
2. Front cushion spring
3. Front fork oil seal
4. Front fork pipe guide
5. Piston stopper ring
6. Fork valve stopper ring
7. Front damper valve
8. Piston stopper ring
9. Front fork piston
10. Fork piston snap ring

and grade of oil (refer to chapter two), and install the top fork bolts before fully tightening the triple clamp pinch-bolts.

CB / CL 350, and CB / CL 450 (except K4 and K5)

Refer to the preceding section on the 125 and 175. Procedures are virtually identical. Before the oil seal circlip can be removed on the 350 and 450, the front fork under cover (CB) or fork boot (CL) must be removed.

SL 350

Refer to the preceding section on the 125 and 175. Procedures are virtually iden-

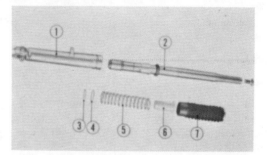

Front fork components; CB and CL 350, and CB and CL 450.

1. Front fork bottom case
2. Front fork pipe
3. 44 mm internal circlip
4. Spring under seat
5. Front cushion spring
6. Front fork under cover guide
7. Front fork boot

tical. Before the fork legs can be withdrawn, both the upper and lower triple clamp pinch-bolts must be loosened. Refer to the accompanying illustrations.

CB 450K4 and K5

DISASSEMBLY

1. Remove the top fork bolts and the piston rod locknuts.

2. Remove the front wheel and fender.

3. Remove the three caliper mounting bolts and the adjuster nut, and lift the caliper assembly away from the fork leg. Do not let the caliper hang by the brake hose; tie it up out of the way with some string or wire.

4. Loosen the upper and lower triple clamp pinch-bolts. Remove the fork legs by pulling gently downward.

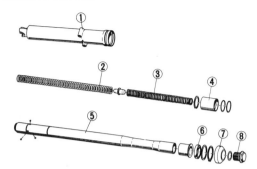

Front fork components, SL 350K1 and K2.

1. Front fork bottom case
2. Front fork cushion spring (B)
3. Front fork cushion spring (A)
4. Front fork piston
5. Front fork pipe
6. Front fork oil seal
7. Front fork dust seal
8. Front fork bolt

5. Pull the spring out of the slider tube and invert the fork leg assembly over a suitable container to drain the oil.

6. Pull the rubber boot off the leg if it remained attached when the leg was removed. Remove the circlip at the top of the lower fork leg, and separate the lower fork leg and slider tube.

7. Pry the seal out of the fork leg, taking care not to damage the inside surface.

8. The damper assembly can be removed from the lower fork leg after unscrewing the allen bolt that is recessed into the bottom of the leg.

INSPECTION

Refer to the preceding section on the 125 and 175.

ASSEMBLY

Assemble in reverse order of disassembly. Observe the following points:

1. Lubricate the seal with oil before installation. If the proper oil seal driver is not available, a piece of wood cut to fit inside the lower fork leg will do the job without damaging the inside surface.

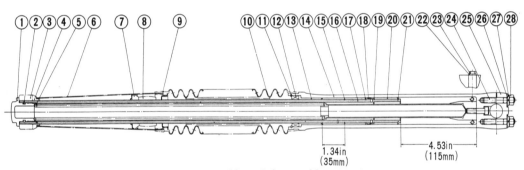

Cross-section of front fork assembly, 450K5.

1. Top bolt	8. Steering stem	15. Travel limit ring	22. Washer
2. O-ring	9. Fork rib	16. Slider tube	23. Bolt
3. Top triple clamp	10. Fork boot	17. Valve limit ring	24. Bolt
4. Fork cover upper cushion	11. Circlip	18. Damper valve	25. Axle clamp
5. Spring cushion	12. Oil seal	19. Piston limit ring	26. Flat washer
6. Fork cover	13. Guide	20. Damper piston	27. Spring washer
7. Fork cover lower cushion	14. Bottom case	21. Piston circlip	28. Nut

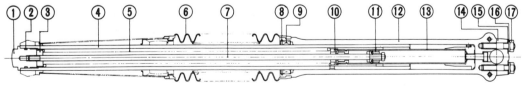

Cross-section of front fork assembly, 450K4.

1. Top bolt	6. Fork boot	11. Collar	16. Spring washer
2. O-ring	7. Damper rod	12. Bottom case	17. Nut
3. Locknut	8. Circlip	13. Damper case	
4. Slider tube	9. Oil seal	14. Axle clamp	
5. Spring	10. Holder	15. Flat washer	

2. Fill the forks with the proper amount and grade of oil (refer to chapter two), and install the top fork bolts before fully tightening the triple clamp pinch-bolts.

3. Adjust the brake caliper after assembly is complete.

STEERING HEAD SERVICE— ALL MODELS

The steering head bearings will not require attention unless a steering fault develops. The procedure for checking the bearings can be found in chapter two.

Disassembly

1. Unscrew the master cylinder mounting bolts and remove the master cylinder from the handlebar (CB 450K4 and K5 only).

2. Disconnect the electrical switches, throttle cable, and clutch and brake cable from the handlebar.

3. Remove the headlight unit from the headlight case and disconnect the wiring at the connectors.

4. Unbolt and remove the handlebar.

5. Loosen the instrument mounting clamp and remove the speedometer/tachometer unit from the upper triple clamp. On models equipped with a steering damper, unscrew the nut at the bottom of the damper and remove the disc, plates, and washer.

6. Remove the front fork assembly.

7. Loosen the center (steering stem) triple clamp pinch-bolt and unscrew the large triple clamp cap nut. Remove the upper triple clamp.

8. The steering stem and lower triple clamp can be withdrawn from the bottom of the steering head after the large steering stem retaining nut is unscrewed. Be careful not to lose the steel balls when removing the steering stem.

Inspection

Examine the steel balls and the bearing races for wear, pitting, and damage. Replace both bearing assemblies if they are not in perfect condition. Make sure that the steering stem is not cracked or bent. If the original bearings are to be reused, clean the races and balls in solvent and dry them thoroughly. If the bearings are to be replaced, drive the races out of the steering head with a soft metal drift. Take care not to damage the inside surface.

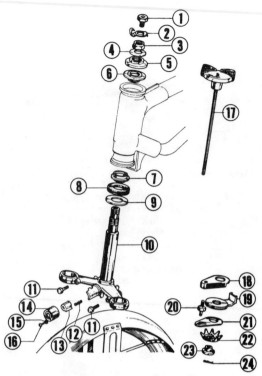

Steering components, 175 shown (typical of all models).

1. Damper lock spring setting bolt
2. Steering damper locking spring
3. Steering head stem nut
4. Steering stem washer
5. Steering head top thread
6. Steering top cone race
7. Steering bottom cone race
8. Steering head dust seal
9. Steering head dust seal washer
10. Steering stem
11. 8 x 32 hex bolt
12. Handle lock spring
13. Handle lock
14. Handle lock case cover
15. 3 mm flat washer
16. 3 x 8 cross screw
17. Steering damper knob
18. Steering damper plate A
19. Steering damper friction disc
20. Friction disc anchor bolt
21. Steering damper plate B
22. Steering damper spring
23. Steering damper nut
24. 6 mm snap-pin

Assembly

Assemble in reverse order of disassembly. Note the following points:

1. Apply a liberal amount of grease to the bearing races. Place the steel balls in the races and install the steering stem.

Take care not to drop the balls as the stem is installed.

2. Tighten the steering stem nut in small increments, checking frequently, until there is no fore-and-aft play at the steering stem and it can move freely and smoothly throughout its travel. Do not overtighten the nut.

Rear Suspension

DeCarbon type shock absorber units are used on all late-model Hondas. These units differ from conventional double-acting hydraulic shocks in that they incorporate a chamber filled with nitrogen gas under high pressure. The pressurized nitrogen effectively prevents the hydraulic fluid from aerating and losing efficiency; however, it also means that the shock absorber cannot be rebuilt because of the danger of explosion. Do not at any time attempt to disassemble the shock absorber, other than to remove the spring.

Metal bushings are used at the swing arm pivot, preventing the swing arm from deflecting when cornering and providing stable handling. The swing arm pivot is provided with grease fittings and, if lubricated regularly, the bushings should never need replacement.

SHOCK ABSORBER AND SPRING REPLACEMENT

The shock absorber/spring unit can be removed after the upper and lower mounting bolts are taken out. To remove the

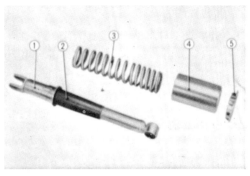

Rear spring/shock absorber components (450 shown).

1. Rear damper assy.
2. Spring guide
3. Rear cushion spring
4. Rear cushion upper case
5. Collar

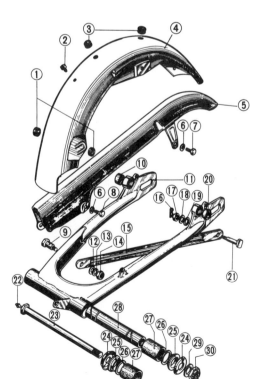

1. Front fuel tank cushion
2. Wire cord grommet
3. Wire cord grommet
4. Rear fender
5. Drive chaincase
6. 6 mm flat washer
7. Bolt
8. Bolt
9. Rear brake stopper arm bolt
10. Rear cushion under rubber bushing
11. Rear fork
12. Spring washer
13. Flat washer
14. Locknut
15. Rear brake stopper arm
16. Lockpin
17. Hex nut
18. Rear fork thrust bushing
19. Spring washer
20. Rear cushion under rubber bushing
21. Rear brake panel stopper bolt
22. Grease nipple
23. Rear fork pivot bolt
24. Rear fork dust-seal cap
25. Rear fork thrust bushing
26. Rear fork felt ring
27. Rear fork pivot bushing
28. Rear fork center collar
29. Rear fork pivot bolt washer
30. Locknut

Swing arm components, 450 shown (typical of all models).

spring, first set the spring adjustment cam in the soft position. Then compress the spring slightly by hand and have a helper remove the split retainer at the top.

To check the effectiveness of the shock absorber, compress and extend it by hand. More resistance should be encountered on the extension stroke than the compression stroke if the shock is operating correctly. Replace if leaking or if the damping is unsatisfactory. Make sure that the spring/shock unit is not binding after it has been reassembled.

SWING ARM PIVOT SERVICE

Disassembly

1. Remove the mufflers.
2. Remove the rear wheel.
3. Remove the rear shock absorber/spring units.
4. Take off the left-side rear crankcase cover (125 and 175 only).

5. Unscrew the swing arm pivot nut and withdraw the pivot shaft. The swing arm can now be separated from the frame.

Inspection

Inspect the swing arm carefully for cracks and distortion. Check to make sure that the pivot shaft is not bent by rolling it on a flat surface. Replace it if bent. Examine the pivot tube (collar) and pivot bushings for damage. If calculated clearance between the pivot tube and bushings exceeds 0.008 in. (0.2 mm), the bushings and tube should be replaced. Check also to make sure that the pivot bolt is a snug fit in the pivot tube.

Assembly

Assembly is a reversal of the disassembly procedures. Liberally grease the pivot tube before installing, and lubricate the pivot at the grease fitting after it is assembled.

9 · Troubleshooting

Introduction

There are certain steps which, if followed, can transform the confusing task of troubleshooting into an exact science. Random efforts often prove frustrating, so a logical method should be adopted. Troubleshooting is nothing more than a systematic process of elimination, tracing back and checking various components until the fault is located. In most cases, this takes very little time and requires very few special tools.

Before you start, try to determine if this is a new problem, or one that's been coming on gradually. If you are an aware rider, you'll know whether or not performance has been diminishing, and consulting the troubleshooting guide in this section may provide an immediate answer. Also, whenever a problem shows up just after work has been done on the bike, check those areas that were involved first, regardless of the nature of the work.

When troubleshooting the engine, you will be concerned with three major areas: the ignition system, the fuel system, and cranking compression pressure. The engine needs spark, fuel, and compression to run, and it will be your job to determine which of these it lacks and why. Let's say that your engine won't start one morning, but it was running fine the night before. The most obvious thing to check first, but which is often overlooked, is the fuel supply. Keep in mind that even if there is gas in the tank, a low supply can sometimes make starting difficult. Check to see if you have fuel at the carburetors by unscrewing one of the float bowl plugs. If so, you can be pretty sure that it is not a lack of fuel that is preventing the engine from starting.

As far as compression is concerned, there are only very few conditions that will cause a sudden loss of compression, and such an occurrence will happen only while the engine is running. You should be able to tell if you have sufficient compression simply by the way the engine sounds and feels as it is cranked over. Or, if you have the spark plugs out, cover the plug hole with your finger and kick the engine over. If the pressure forces your finger off the hole, there should be enough compression for the engine to start. Of course, the most accurate way to check compression is by using a compression gauge.

So, you have found that the engine has relatively normal compression and is getting fuel. The final area of investigation is the electrical system. Check to see if you are getting spark to the cylinders by removing the plug leads, one at a time, and inserting a metal object such as a nail into the plug connectors. Using a piece of rubber as insulation, hold the nail about $\frac{1}{8}$ in. from the engine and crank it over with the ignition on. If you have spark at the leads, remove and check the spark plugs. If not, trace the ignition system back with a test light (simply a 12 volt bulb and battery with two wires attached, used to check electrical continuity). Start by checking for electricity at the points while they are open. If you have juice there, the problem lies in the coil, spark plug wires, or the wires between the coil and points. If you find that there is no supply of electricity to the coil, start looking for loose connectors in the wiring between the coil and ignition switch. Speaking of connectors, whenever you have a problem with the electrical system, they are the first things you should examine. These little devils have the habit of vibrating and pulling loose for no particular reason, and cause far more trouble and aggravation than any other part of the electrical system.

If you have a charging system problem, the most common faults to look for are loose connectors or a loose rectifier mounting nut. A large percentage of charging system troubles stem from these minor faults.

All of the above can be considered troubleshooting the engine to get it running, not troubleshooting to cure running faults. Once you have found the general location of the trouble, it is usually quite simple to make pinpoint checks or temporarily substitute new parts to determine exactly where the problem lies. The most important thing to remember is to try to remain rational and approach the troubleshooting procedure logically. If you do this, chances are you will find what you are looking for and save yourself some time, money, aggravation, and embarrassment (when the mechanic tells you that you pushed the bike four miles and paid him five dollars to replace a fuse).

Troubleshooting an engine that is running poorly is often a bit trickier than trying to determine why an engine won't start. You will still be involved with the compression, fuel system, and electrical system of your engine, but the problems will be more subtle and harder to detect. It pays here, if you are making adjustments or fine-tuning, to make one adjustment at a time, thoroughly check the results, and record the findings. Otherwise you will confuse yourself, ruin the results of one adjustment with another, and accomplish nothing.

Assuming that your engine has not expired with a big bang, any mechanical difficulties that you suspect will have taken some time to develop and are most often related to wear. Try to remember if a new sound shortly preceded the trouble, as sounds can often help trace the problems. (Don't become paranoid about "new" noises though, because you can imagine all kinds of terrible sounds if you really try.)

Remember, when you are trying to diagnose a running fault, to check all the parts related to the component you are examining. For example, suppose you are carefully scrutinizing a carburetor, expecting a revelation at any moment. In the meantime, don't forget to check the intake tube clamps, the air filter, and the fuel filter to make sure that the carburetor is not being sabotaged in one way or another by these associated components (too much air, or too little air or fuel). Or, if you are busy getting zapped by the high tension lead while checking for sufficient spark, don't forget to check that the plug connector is tightly attached to the wire, that the wire insulation is not worn or cracked, etc., etc. Look for the little things, and do it systematically and thoroughly. In many cases, a qualified mechanic may be able to help you with a specific problem without even having to look at the bike. He's seen it all before, so don't hesitate to ask. The worst it can get you is a service appointment for next week.

Engine Noises

One of the first indications of change in the condition of your motorcycle is the sound that emanates from it. A thoughtful rider will know that something is going wrong long before it happens and may be able to rectify the situation before it leads to costly repairs. Every machine has its own sounds and these sounds will remain constant until something begins to go wrong. Pay attention to this and whenever a new sound appears, seek consultation from a qualified mechanic who's heard them all before

Valve Clatter

When tappet adjustment time rolls around, you'll know it because the valves will let you know. They always make some noise, especially when cold, but will really get noisy when in need of attention. When listening to the tappets, keep in mind that when you can hear them, chances are they're alright. If you can't hear anything as soon as you start the bike, they're too tight and will cause damage to the valve train.

Pinging

Poor quality gasoline, advanced ignition timing, incorrect spark plug heat range, or a piece of metal or carbon in the combustion chamber can be causes of pinging.

Pinging sounds are generally associated with the top end, and occur at middle range speeds during acceleration. Most of the time it is caused by pre-ignition due to the use of low octane fuel in a high compression engine. These unnecessary detonations cause undue strain on piston assemblies and bearings.

If the ignition timing is advanced too far, the force of the combustion will try to force the piston down before it completes its rotation. This is another type of pre-ignition and is as harmful as the use of poor fuel. When pistons end up with holes in them, it is usually because of this.

If the spark plug in use is too hot, it can't dissipate its heat quickly enough and begins to act like a glow plug. This causes pre-ignition also and can be corrected by using a colder plug.

Carbon or metal pieces in the combustion chamber can heat up and act like a glow plug. This is less common than the others and only occurs when the engine is running hot. The only way to quiet this type of pinging is through top end surgery.

Piston Slap

Slap occurs most often at mid-throttle range during acceleration and requires top end disassembly to eliminate it. The noise is metallic and is caused by excessive piston-cylinder clearance. If the noise goes away after the engine warms up, the condition is not urgent but you'd better start planning on rebuilding the top end quite soon.

Knock

If you hear a mighty knocking noise coming from the bottom end while accelerating, you can be pretty sure the main bearings haven't long to go. It also may be a crankshaft problem and is remedied in either case by taking down the entire engine.

Rap

When the connecting rod bearings start to go, rap develops. This is most often heard during deceleration and increases in intensity with the speed of the engine.

Double Rap

This is caused by excessive piston–piston pin clearance and is most noticeable as a quick succession of raps at idle speeds.

Whine

In the overhead cam Honda engines, an unusually loud whine often indicates a loose cam chain. Adjustment should eliminate the noise. Refer to chapter three.

Engine Troubleshooting

Problem—Engine fails to start

Probable Causes	Inspection and Remedy
Fuel starvation	Check fuel supply. Check to see that the fuel tap is turned on. Check the fuel filter and lines for obstruction.
Fuel flooding	Remove and dry spark plugs. Check the carburetor float needle and seat for dirt and wear, and check the float level. Refer to chapter 6, "Carburetor Overhaul" section.
Insufficiently charged battery	Check electrolyte level and recharge battery. Investigate the cause of battery discharging. Refer to chapter 7, "Charging System."
Fouled or improperly gapped spark plugs	Clean and gap, or replace. Refer to chapter 3, "Spark Plug" section.
Badly oxidized, dirty, or improperly gapped ignition points	Clean and gap, or replace ignition points and condensers. Refer to chapter 3, "Contact Breaker Points" section.
Spark plug cables damaged	Replace high-tension wiring harness.
Ignition timing out of adjustment	Reset timing, refer to chapter 3, "Ignition Timing" section.
Loose connection in ignition system	Check wiring harness connections.
Ignition coil defective	Make sure that the ignition points, low-tension wires, and high-tension wires are in good condition. Check coil spark by inserting a metal object, such as a nail, into one of the spark plug wire connectors, holding it about $\frac{1}{4}$ in. from the engine (with a cloth or other insulating material to prevent shock) and cranking the engine over with the ignition on. (The battery should have close to its normal amount of charge.) The coil should produce a fat, hot, consistent spark. Lack of spark or weak spark indicates a defective coil.
Battery terminals loose or corroded	Clean and tighten.
Low compression	If the engine can be turned over on the kick-starter with less than normal effort, perform a compression test and determine the cause of low compression. Refer to chapter 3, "Compression Check" section.

Problem—Engine hard to start

Probable Causes	Inspection and Remedy
Fuel starvation	Check fuel level. A minimal-amount of fuel in the tank can sometimes make starting hard. Check float level. Refer to chapter 6 "Carburetor Overhaul" section. Make sure fuel tank breather is not blocked. Check fuel filter for obstruction. Check for intake air leaks. Make sure that the intake tube clamps are tight.
Weak spark	Check ignition points, coil, ignition wires, and spark plugs as described in chapter 3.
Contaminated fuel	Drain and replace the gas in the float bowls and fuel tank.
Battery charge low	Check electrolyte level and recharge the battery. If discharging persists, investigate the cause. Refer to chapter 7 "Charging System."
Ignition timing improperly adjusted	Check and adjust timing. Refer to chapter 3, "Ignition Timing" section.
Low compression	If the engine can be turned over on the kick-starter with less than normal effort, perform a compression test and determine the cause of low compression. Refer to chapter 3, "Compression Check" section.

Problem—Engine dies while running

Probable Causes	Inspection and Remedy
Lack of fuel	Check fuel supply. Check fuel lines and carburetors for leaking. Check fuel lines and fuel filter for obstructions.
Lack of spark	Check electrical overload fuse that is located near the battery. Check ignition wiring harness connectors.

Engine Troubleshooting

Problem—Engine dies while running

Probable Causes	Inspection and Remedy
Lack of spark	Check battery terminal connections and ground cable frame connection. Check charging system wire connections and make sure that the rectifier mounting nut is tight.

Problem—Engine idles poorly

Probable Causes	Inspection and Remedy
Mechanical failure	If the engine stops with a bang while running, it is time to thoroughly inspect your warranty policy and/or bank balance.
Improper fuel mixture	Adjust carburetor air screws properly. Refer to chapter 3, "Carburetor Adjustment" section. Remove and clean carburetor low-speed jets. Refer to chapter 6, "Carburetor Overhaul" section. Check float level. Refer to chapter 6, "Carburetor Overhaul" section. Check for intake air leaks. Make sure that the mounting bolts are tight.
Carburetors not synchronized properly	Refer to chapter 3, "Carburetor Synchronization" section.
Weak spark	Check the spark plugs. Clean and gap, or replace if necessary. Check ignition points. Clean and gap, or replace if necessary, and set ignition timing. Refer to chapter 3. Check spark plug wires for worn or cracked insulation. Check the connectors for cracks and make sure they are securely attached.
Valve sticking at low speeds	Check and adjust valve clearances if necessary. Refer to chapter 3, "Valve Adjustment" section. Use a supplemental lubricant such as a top cylinder oil to free the valve.

Problem—Engine runs poorly at low to mid-range throttle openings

Probable Causes	Inspection and Remedy
Fuel mixture too lean	Check for intake air leaks. Make sure that the carburetor jet needles are positioned correctly. Refer to chapter 6. Check for fuel contamination by draining the float bowl(s) and watching for water. Check spark plugs, ignition points, ignition wires and connectors, and coil output. Check ignition timing and advance unit. Refer to chapter 3.

Problem—Engine misfires and runs poorly at full throttle

Probable Causes	Inspection and Remedy
Improper fuel mixture	Clean air filter element. Check for fuel line or fuel filter obstruction. Check float level. Refer to chapter 6, "Carburetor Overhaul" section. Check for intake air leaks. Make sure that the main jets are not loose and that they are the right size. Refer to chapter 6.
Fouled or worn spark plugs	Carbon-fouled plugs, or old plugs, can sometimes cause high-speed misfire even though they look usable. If in doubt, try a new set. Make sure that you are using the correct heat range. Refer to chapter 3, "Spark Plug" section.
Ignition advance unit faulty	Check ignition timing with a strobe light. If the advance unit is not functioning properly, disassemble and inspect it. Refer to chapter 3, "Ignition Timing" section.
Weak spark	Check the ignition points and replace them, in any case, if they have been in service for more than 5,000 miles. Check coil output, ignition wires, and spark plug connectors. Refer to chapter 3.

Problem—Loss of compression and power

Probable Causes	Inspection and Remedy
Mechanical wear or failure, burnt valves, leaking head gasket, etc.	Refer to chapter 3, "Compression Check," for analysis of compression test results.

Engine Troubleshooting

Problem—Backfiring

Probable Causes	Inspection and Remedy
Lean fuel mixture	Check for intake air leaks and exhaust leaks.
Improper ignition timing	Check and adjust ignition timing. Make sure that the ignition advance unit is functioning properly. Refer to chapter 3, "Ignition Timing" section.

Problem—Overheating, accompanied by pinging or spark knock

Probable Causes	Inspection and Remedy
Ignition timing incorrect	Adjust.
Contaminated or poor quality gasoline	Drain float bowls and fuel tank. Refill with fresh gas.
Fuel mixture too rich	Examine and clean air filter element, if necessary. Check for worn main jet tube and jet needle. Make sure the needle is correctly positioned. Refer to chapter 6, "Carburetor Overhaul" section.
Weak spark	Check battery terminal connections and battery charge. Refer to chapter 2, "Battery Section," and chapter 7, "Charging System."
Lack of oil pressure, oil not circulating	Remove and overhaul oil pump. Refer to chapter 3.
Excessive carbon buildup in combustion chambers and on piston crowns	Perform a top end overhaul. Refer to chapter 4.
Incorrect spark plug heat range	Check for proper spark plugs in chapter 3, "Spark Plug" and "Specification" sections.
Lean fuel mixture	Check for intake air leaks.
Lack of engine oil	Shame on you.

Problem—Excessive oil consumption

Probable Causes	Inspection and Remedy
Mechanical wear, piston, failure, etc.	Perform a compression test and analysis. Refer to chapter 3, "Compression Check" section. If compression pressure is normal, oil burning is probably the fault of defective valve seals or worn valve guides.
Engine breather obstructed	Inspect and clean breather outlet.

Problem—Excessive vibration

Probable Causes	Inspection and Remedy
Engine mounts loose or broken	Inspect and secure. Refer to chapter 4, "Engine Removal and Installation" section.
Incorrect ignition timing	Check and adjust.
Misfiring, loss of compression, tight or sticking valves	Perform a tune-up.

Clutch Troubleshooting

Problem—Clutch slippage

Probable Causes	Inspection and Remedy
Improper adjustment	Perform full clutch adjustment. Refer to chapter 2, "Clutch" section.
Weak springs	Overhaul clutch unit. Refer to chapter 4, "Clutch" section.
Worn or glazed discs	See above.

Problem—Clutch chatter

Probable Causes	Inspection and Remedy
Weak springs	Overhaul clutch unit.
Warped plates	See above.
Warped pressure plate	See above.
Pressure plate rivets loose	See above.

Clutch Troubleshooting

Problem—Clutch drag

Probable Causes	Inspection and Remedy
Improper adjustment	Perform full clutch adjustment. Refer to chapter 2, "Clutch" section.
Warped plates	Overhaul clutch unit.
Defective release mechanism	Inspect and replace parts as necessary.

Transmission Troubleshooting

Problem—Hard gear shifting

Probable Causes	Inspection and Remedy
Improper clutch adjustment	Perform full clutch adjustment. Refer to chapter 2, "Clutch" section.
Damaged shift forks or drum	Overhaul shifter mechanism. Refer to chapter 4, "Shifter Mechanism Service."
Mainshaft and countershaft improperly aligned	Disassemble the transmission and replace the shafts or bearings as necessary. Refer to chapter 4, "Transmission Service" section.

Problem—Excessive gear noise

Probable Causes	Inspection and Remedy
Excessive backlash	Disassemble the transmission and check gear backlash. Refer to chapter 4, "Transmission Service" section.
Worn mainshaft or counter-shaft bearings	Overhaul the transmission unit. Refer to chapter 4.

Problem—Transmission jumps out of gear

Probable Causes	Inspection and Remedy
Worn shift forks or drum	Overhaul shifter mechanism. Refer to chapter 4, "Shifter Mechanism Service" section.
Worn splines on countershaft or mainshaft, worn gears	Overhaul the transmission. Refer to chapter 4, "Transmission Service."

Electrical System Troubleshooting

Complete testing, diagnosis, and repair procedures for the electrical system components will be found in chapter 7.

Hydraulic Disc Brake Troubleshooting

Problem—Excessive lever travel and loss of braking power

Probable Causes	Inspection and Remedy
Air in hydraulic system	Bleed the brake as described in chapter 8, "Front Brake" section.
Leak in master cylinder or caliper, as evidenced by fluid loss	Overhaul faulty component as described in chapter 8, "Front Brake" section.
Worn disc pads	Check pad wear and replace as described in chapter 8.

Problem—Brake squeal

Probable Causes	Inspection and Remedy
Glazed pads	Lightly sand the disc pads and use the brake gently for a hundred miles or so until they have a chance to bed in properly.
Improperly adjusted caliper	Adjust the caliper as described in chapter 8, "Front Brake Adjustment" section.
Extremely dusty or dirty front brake assembly	Clean with water. Do not use high-pressure spray equipment.

Hydraulic Disc Brake Troubleshooting

Problem—Brake shudder

Probable Causes	Inspection and Remedy
Warped disc	Replace as described in chapter 8.
Distorted pads	See above.
Oil or break fluid impregnated pads	See above.

Appendix

Honda Service Tools

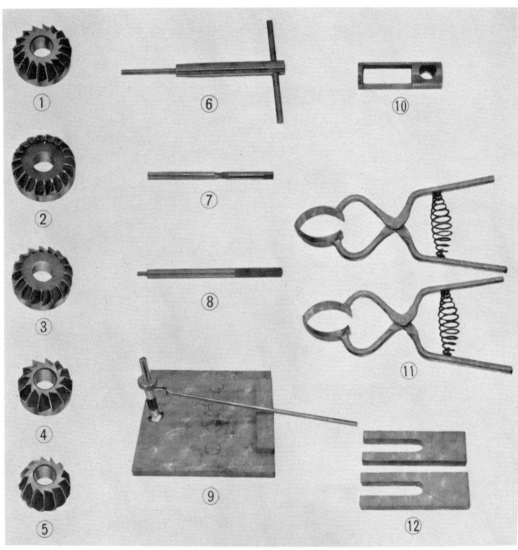

REF NO.	TOOL NO.	DESCRIPTION
	07000–32301	Special Tool Set for CB 500
①	07001–32301	Valve seat 90° cutter
②	07003–32301	Intake valve seat top cutter
③	07004–32301	Exhaust valve seat top cutter
④	07005–32301	Intake valve seat interior cutter
⑤	07006–32301	Exhaust valve seat interior cutter
⑥	07007–32301	Valve seat cutter holder
⑦	07008–32301	Valve guide reamer
⑧	07046–32301	Valve guide driving and removing tool
⑨	07031–30011	Valve spring compresser
⑩	07031–32301	Valve spring compresser attachment
⑪	07032–32301	Piston ring compresser (2 pcs)
⑫	07033–55101	Piston base (2 pcs)
—	07001–32301	Valve seat cutter set
—	07997–05101	Valve seat cutter case

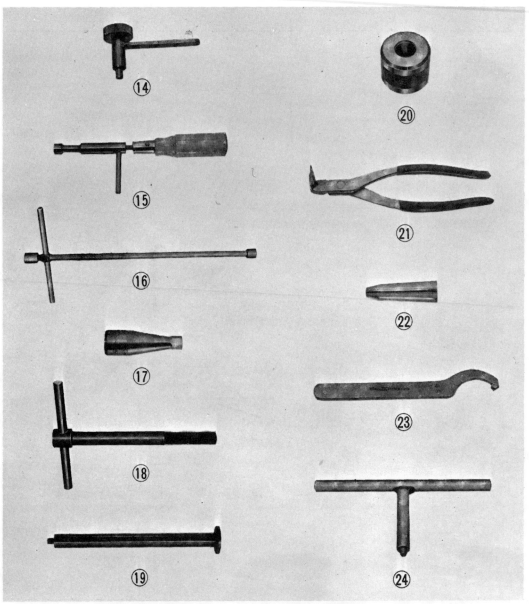

REF NO.	TOOL NO.	DESCRIPTION
⑭	07081–32301	Valve tappet locknut wrench
⑮	07087–32301	Carburetor synchronization adjusting wrench
⑯	07078–32301	12 mm cylinder head nut wrench
⑰	07094–32301	Spark plug wrench
⑱	07011–21601	Alternator rotor puller
⑲	07009–32301	Slide hammer shaft (primary shaft remover)
⑳	07009–32305	Weight
㉑	07073–32301	Master cylinder circlip pliers
㉒	07043–32301	Piston cup guide
㉓	07072–20001	Pin wrench
㉔	07085–32301	Allen wrench
—	07043–32305	Master cylinder piston guide

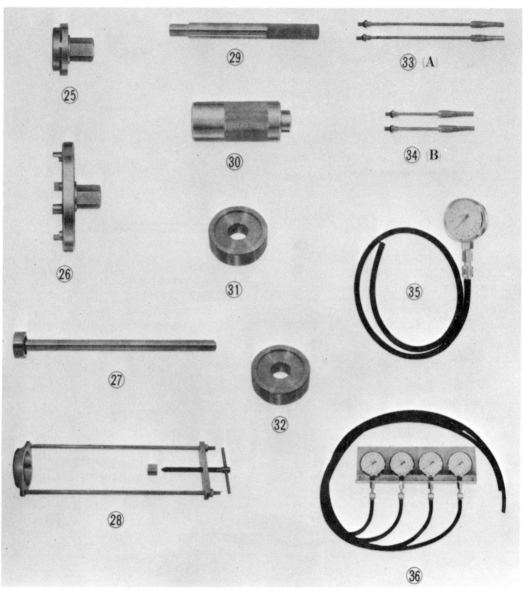

REF NO.	TOOL NO.	DESCRIPTION
25	07088–32301	Bearing retainer wrench (front)
26	07088–32305	Bearing retainer wrench (rear)
27	07034–32301	Front fork assembling bar
28	07035–30001	Rear spring removal tool
29	07048–32301	Bearing driver
30	07048–32320	Bearing driver
31	07048–32305	Bearing driver attachment
32	07048–32315	Bearing driver attachment
33	07068–30007	Vacuum gauge attachment (2 pcs)
34	07068–30010	Vacuum gauge attachment (2 pcs)
35	07064–30012	Vacuum gauge
36	07064–30001	Vacuum gauge set
—	07790–29201	Tool case
—	07065–30001	Pressure gauge
—	07068–30001	Oil pressure gauge attachment

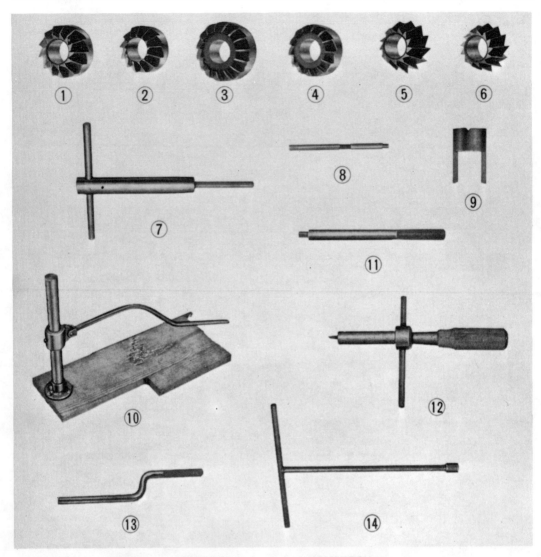

REF NO.	TOOL NO.	DESCRIPTION
	07000–30011	Special Tool Set for CB 750
①	07001–30001	Intake valve seat 90° cutter
②	07002–30001	Exhaust valve seat 90° cutter
③	07003–30001	Intake valve seat top cutter
④	07004–30001	Exhaust valve seat top cutter
⑤	07005–30001	Intake valve seat interior cutter
⑥	07006–30001	Exhaust valve seat interior cutter
⑦	07007–30001	Valve seat cutter holder
⑧	07008–30001	Valve guide reamer
⑨	07031–30001	Valve remover attachment
⑩	07031–30010	Valve remover body
⑪	07046–30001	Valve guide driving & removing tool
⑫	07087–30001	Valve tappet locknut wrench
⑬	07050–30001	Valve rocker arm shaft removing tool
⑭	07078–30001	Cylinder head bolt wrench

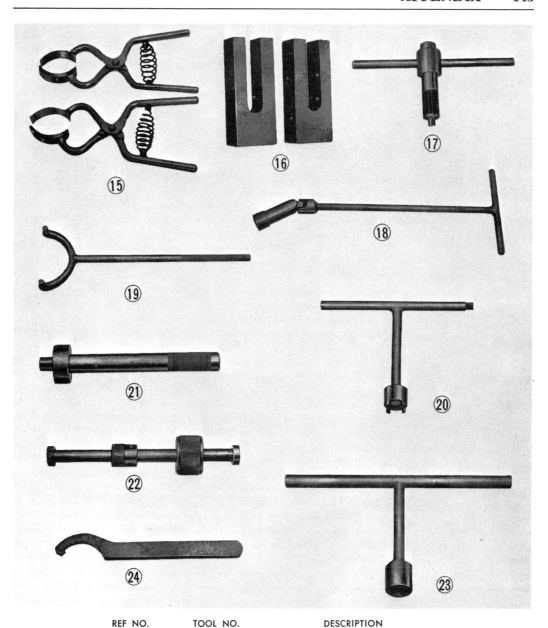

REF NO.	TOOL NO.	DESCRIPTION
⑮	07032–30001	Piston ring compresser
⑯	07033–30001	Piston base (2 pcs)
⑰	07011–30001	Alternator rotor puller
⑱	07094–30002	Spark plug wrench
⑲	07022–30001	Drive sprocket holder
⑳	07086–30001	Clutch locknut wrench
㉑	07048–30020	Countershaft bearing driving tool
㉒	07048–30025	Countershaft bearing removing tool
㉓	07083–21601	Stem nut box wrench
㉔	07072–20001	Pin wrench

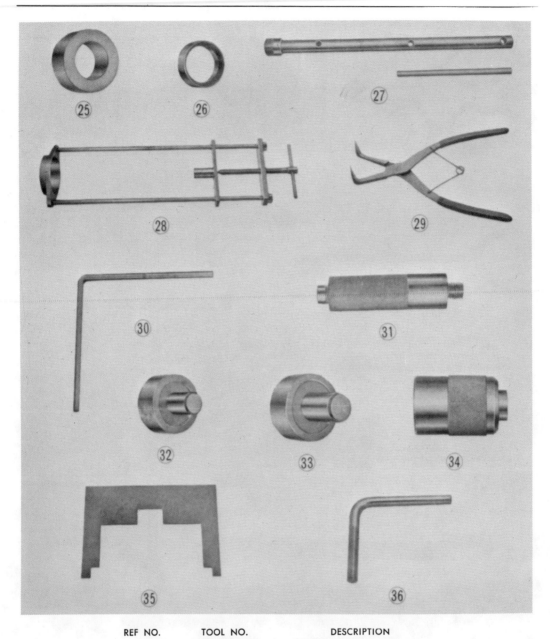

REF NO.	TOOL NO.	DESCRIPTION
25	07057–29201	Front fork oil seal driving weight
26	07054–30001	Front fork oil seal driving guide
27	07034–30001	Front fork assembling bar
28	07035–30001	Rear spring removal tool
29	07073–30001	Master cylinder circlip pliers
30	07080–30001	Allen wrench
31	07096–30001	Bearing driver handle
32	07048–30001	Front wheel bearing driver
33	07048–30005	Rear wheel bearing driver
34	07048–30015	Final drive shaft bearing driver
35	07144–99962	Carburetor float level gauge
36	07063–30001	Crankshaft turning handle

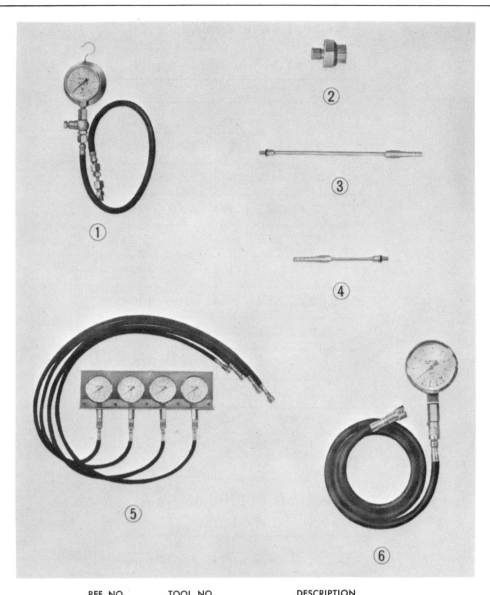

REF NO.	TOOL NO.	DESCRIPTION
1	07065–30001	Oil pressure gauge (10 kg)
2	07068–30001	Oil pressure gauge adaptor
3	07068–30007	Vacuum gauge attachment (2 pcs)
4	07068–30012	Vacuum gauge attachment (2 pcs)
5	07064–30001	Vacuum gauge set (4 pcs)
6	07064–30010	Vacuum gauge

Metric Conversion Charts

Inches to Millimeters—Units

Inches	0	10	20	30	40
0		254.0	508.0	762.0	1016.0
1	25.4	279.4	533.4	787.4	1041.4
2	50.8	304.8	558.8	812.8	1066.8
3	76.2	330.2	584.2	838.2	1092.2
4	101.6	355.6	609.6	863.6	1117.6
5	127.0	381.0	635.0	889.0	1143.0
6	152.4	406.4	660.4	914.4	1168.4
7	177.8	431.8	685.8	939.8	1193.8
8	203.2	457.2	711.2	965.2	1219.2
9	228.6	482.6	736.6	990.6	1244.6

One Inch—25.399978 millimeters
One Meter—39.370113 inches
One Mile—1.6093 Km
One Km—.62138 mile

Decimals to Millimeters— Fractions

1/1000		1/100		1/10	
inches	mm	inches	mm	inches	mm
.001	.0254	.01	.254	.1	2.54
.002	.0508	.02	.508	.2	5.08
.003	.0762	.03	.726	.3	7.62
.004	.1016	.04	1.016	.4	10.16
.005	.1270	.05	1.270	.5	12.70
.006	.1524	.06	1.524	.6	15.24
.007	.1778	.07	1.778	.7	17.78
.008	.2032	.08	2.032	.8	20.32
.009	.2286	.09	2.286	.9	22.86

Millimeters to Inches—Units

mm	0	10	20	30	40
0		.39370	.78740	1.18110	1.57480
1	.03937	.43307	.82677	1.22047	1.61417
2	.07874	.47244	.86614	1.25984	1.65354
3	.11811	.51181	.90551	1.29921	1.69291
4	.15748	.55118	.94488	1.33858	1.73228
5	.19685	.59055	.98425	1.37795	1.77165
6	.23622	.62992	1.02362	1.41732	1.81103
7	.27559	.66929	1.06299	1.45669	1.85040
8	.31496	.70866	1.10236	1.49606	1.88977
9	.35433	.74803	1.14173	1.53543	1.92914

mm	50	60	70	80	90
0	1.96851	2.36221	2.75591	3.14961	3.54331
1	2.00788	2.40158	2.79528	3.18891	3.58268
2	2.04725	2.44095	2.83465	3.22835	3.62205
3	2.08662	2.48032	2.87402	3.26772	3.66142
4	2.12599	2.51969	2.91339	3.30709	3.70079
5	2.16536	2.55906	2.95276	3.34646	3.74016
6	2.20473	2.59843	2.99213	3.38583	3.77953
7	2.24410	2.63780	3.03150	3.42520	3.81890
8	2.28347	2.67717	3.07087	3.46457	3.85827
9	2.32284	2.71654	3.11024	3.50394	3.89764

Millimeters to Inches—
Fractions

1/1000		1/100		1/10	
mm	inches	mm	inches	mm	inches
0.001	.000039	0.01	.00039	0.1	.00394
0.002	.000079	0.02	.00079	0.2	.00787
0.003	.000118	0.03	.00118	0.3	.01181
0.004	.000157	0.04	.00157	0.4	.01575
0.005	.000197	0.05	.00197	0.5	.01969
0.006	.000236	0.06	.00236	0.6	.02362
0.007	.000276	0.07	.00276	0.7	.02756
0.008	.000315	0.08	.00315	0.8	.03150
0.009	.000354	0.09	.00354	0.9	.03543

Degree Wheel

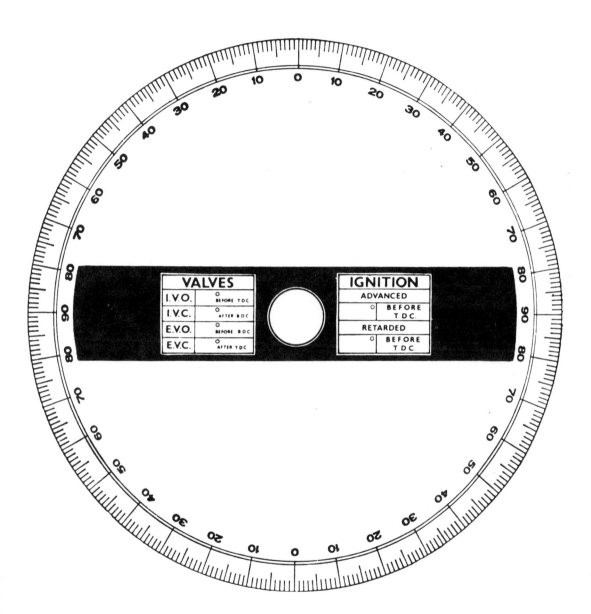

VALVES	
I.V.O.	° BEFORE T D C
I.V.C.	° AFTER B D C
E.V.O.	° BEFORE B D C
E.V.C.	° AFTER T D C

IGNITION	
ADVANCED	
°	BEFORE T.D.C.
RETARDED	
°	BEFORE T.D.C.